FOR LIFE AND LIBERTY

The Story of the Declaration of Independence

The courageous patriots representing the 13 British colonies in America—men like George Washington, Benjamin Franklin, Thomas Jefferson, John Adams, Roger Sherman, Patrick Henry—called the First Continental Congress to express their grievances, not to break with Britain. They protested taxation without representation, denial of trial by jury, quartering of troops in peacetime, restraint of free trade. Though they wanted the right to shape their own destinies, only provocation beyond endurance could lead the patriots to declare their independence from the mother country and to set up their own government. After the gunfire at Lexington and Concord, the slaughter on Bunker Hill, the bombardment of Charleston, a Second Continental Congress convened and the Declaration of Independence was signed on July 4, 1776. Thus the course of history was changed for all time.

Books by Mary Hoehling

Girl Soldier and Spy
Sarah Emma Edmundson

The Real Sherlock Holmes
Arthur Conan Doyle

Yankee in the White House
John Quincy Adams

FOR LIFE AND LIBERTY

The Story of the Declaration of Independence

by
Mary Hoehling
and
Betty Randall

"Rebellion to tyrants is obedience to God"

JULIAN MESSNER
NEW YORK

Published simultaneously in the United States and Canada by
Julian Messner, a division of Simon & Schuster, Inc.,
1 West 39 Street, New York, N.Y. 10018. All right reserved.

Copyright, ©, 1969 by Mary Hoehling and Betty Randall

Lines by Robert Frost from "For John F. Kennedy
His Inauguration" from IN THE CLEARING by Robert Frost.
Copyright © 1961, 1962 by Robert Frost. Reprinted
by permission of Holt, Rinehart and Winston, Inc.

Printed in the United States of America

SBN 671-32099-8 Cl. Tr.
671-32101-3 MCE

Library of Congress Catalog Card No. 69-12106

CONTENTS

	PROLOGUE	9
I.	THE FLAME IS LIT	13
	"For opposing . . . his invasions on the rights of the people . . ."	
II.	TWOPENNY TREASON	23
	"He has refused his assent to laws . . . wholesome and necessary for the public good."	
III.	THE SONS OF LIBERTY	33
	". . . For imposing Taxes on us without our Consent . . ."	
IV.	THE TRUMPET SOUNDS	45
	". . . to secure these rights . . ."	
V.	REBELLION POSTPONED	56
	". . . Governments are instituted . . . , deriving their just powers from the consent of the governed . . ."	
VI.	THE GOOD SHIP LIBERTY	66
	"He has dissolved Representative Houses . . ."	
VII.	NONE BUT A SLAVE	75
	". . . For depriving us . . . of trial by jury . . ."	
VIII.	THE GATHERING STORM	84
	"He has kept among us, in times of peace, Standing Armies . . ."	

IX.	A SALTY BREW ". . . For . . . altering fundamentally the Forms of our Governments . . ."	93
X.	A NURSERY OF AMERICAN STATESMEN ". . . For abolishing the free System of English Laws in a neighboring Province . . ."	103
XI.	LIBERTY OR DEATH ". . For cutting off our Trade with all parts of the world . . ."	115
XII.	A HOUSE DIVIDED "He has . . . ravaged our Coasts, burnt our towns . . ."	126
XIII.	INDEPENDENCE LIKE A TORRENT "He has abdicated Government here, by declaring us out of his Protection and waging War against us."	140
XIV.	PHILADELPHIA, JULY 3, 1776 "When in the course of human events . . ."	154
XV.	JULY 4, 1776 ". . . We . . . pledge . . . our sacred Honor."	166

EPILOGUE	176
THE DECLARATION OF INDEPENDENCE	181
BIBLIOGRAPHY	186
INDEX	188

FOR LIFE AND LIBERTY

The Story of the Declaration of
Independence

PROLOGUE

FOR over 150 years, men and women from the British Isles and Europe had been braving 3,000 miles of treacherous, storm-racked ocean to cling to the edge of a continent inhabited by savages—for the sake of freedom.

These refugees from political and religious oppression, from war and poverty, were a motley group of dreamers and adventurers, malcontents and idealists, peasants and noblemen. On a narrow strip of land bordering that "uncouth, huge and monstrous wilderness" that was America, they were building a new world for a new kind of people.

Most of Britain's colonies were established by royal charter. They were governed by royal appointees, subject to British laws, dependent on the mother country for supplies and for trade. Britain's armies protected the colonies from domination by the French and from Indian attack.

By the mid-eighteenth century, Britain's Atlantic colonies had burgeoned into thriving communities. The total population of one million and a half was primarily native-born, young, male, aggressive. Mobility, both social and geographical, marked this new society of transplanted Englishmen.

The yeoman, who had always paid his tithe to the manor lord, owned his own land in America. Even those who came as bonded servants moved on to their own farms or set up their own businesses when they had worked off their "indentures." There was no limit to the wealth and position a man might achieve in America if he had courage and initiative and was willing to work.

The very earth and trees of this new world seemed to exude a spirit of independence and freedom. In 1748, Peter Kalm, a visiting university professor from Sweden, observed:

"It is . . . of great advantage to the crown of England that the North American colonies are near a country under the government of the French . . . for the English colonies in this part of the world have increased so much in their number of inhabitants, and in their riches, that they almost vie with Old England."

Now, in order to keep control of the wealth and trade of these lusty offspring, Britain's government tried to impose on the colonists the very strictures that had caused their forefathers and them to emigrate from their homelands.

"They are forbidden to establish new manufactures which would turn to the disadvantage of the British commerce," observed young Peter Kalm. "They are not allowed to dig for any gold or silver, unless they send them to England immediately; they have not the liberty of trading to any parts that do not belong to the British dominions, and foreign traders are not allowed to send their ships to them. These and some other restrictions occasion the inhabitants of the English colonies to grow less tender for their mother country.

"I have been told by Englishmen," the visitor concluded, "that the English colonies of North America, in the space of thirty or fifty years, would be able to form a state by themselves, entirely independent of Old England."

Peter Kalm's prediction proved amazingly accurate. During the next twenty-five years, Great Britain tried to make the American colonies share some part of the burden of imperial expenses—at least to pay the cost of their own government and defense. But the duties and taxes imposed by the home government caused increasing resentment in the colonies, which burst forth ultimately in riots and, finally, open rebellion.

The chief grievance underlying colonial resistance to Great Britain was the levying of duties and taxes by a parliament in which the colonies were "without representation," and the making of laws without the "consent of the governed."

As loyal subjects of the Crown of England, the colonists made many efforts to effect reconciliation—efforts that were largely ignored by Britain, or answered with further restraints imposed by a faraway government that looked upon the colonies as "insignificant offspring."

Loyalty to Great Britain and internal dissension among the colonies defeated early attempts to unite in a common cause, and final severing of those ties of brotherhood that bound the Atlantic colonies to the motherland, Great Britain, came gradually, painfully. But by 1774, as the mailed hand of royal power tightened round the American colonies, the spark of self-determination exploded into flame. The word "independence," heretofore only whispered, swelled to a roar.

The first illegal Continental Congress was called only to draft a resolution of grievances. Yet, even as the delegates sweltered over their task in Philadelphia, more British soldiers, and hired German mercenaries, were landed on colonial shores—not to guard them against enemy attack, but to fight the colonists themselves.

Before the Second Continental Congress convened in the autumn of 1775, rebellion flared into open warfare. An infant nation had been spawned in bloody anguish—at Lexington, Concord and Bunker Hill—as British soldier and British subject opened fire on each other.

Separation from Great Britain became the rallying cry of the United Colonies, for it seemed now a fact, needing only a formal declaration of independence.

The drafting and signing of the Declaration of Independence by the chosen representatives of the thirteen colonies on July 4, 1776, marked the official birth of the new nation. The United States of America had come into being, and the world would never be the same.

This was, indeed, a turning point in history.

I

THE FLAME IS LIT

> *"For opposing . . . his invasions on the rights of the people . . ."*

IN America even a farmer's son like John Adams could go to college, though at Harvard he had ranked twenty-fifth in his class of fifty—on the basis of social position rather than scholastic merit. John Adams was twenty-four in 1761 and had just begun to practice law in Braintree in The Massachusetts Bay Colony when he traveled to Boston to hear James Otis argue against the writs of assistance.

It was a damp February day, and the snow lay deep on the cobblestone pavement, muffling the clatter of drays and coaches in the twisted narrow streets. Market men and women crying their wares near Faneuil Hall shivered in the icy wind. The smell of fish and the sea mingled in the frosty air with the pungent odors of horses and nightsoil.

Walking along King Street, Adams saw marks of the great fire of 1760. Many had compared it to the blaze that had destroyed London a hundred years before. New England's largest port was built of wood, and seemed always to be on fire. Tile or slate roofs had been decreed in Town Meeting after the latest conflagration almost demolished the city. Some favored building only with brick, as in Philadelphia and Charles Town, South Carolina. These ports to the south were beginning to overshadow Boston. During the past ten years Philadelphia and New York had surged ahead in population and commerce.

Everywhere Adams saw signs of depression. Too many shops along Orange and Newbury streets stood empty and shuttered. Too many bare-masted ships were warped to silent wharves, for the end of the French and Indian War had curtailed trade throughout the colonies.

When John Adams was admitted to the bar in 1758, he had found the clangor of the busy port jarring. Great Britain then had been in the midst of a great war for her empire. Boston was a peninsula nearly encircled by its harbor, and every wharf was a bustle of activity. That September, Lord Jeffrey Amherst sailed in aboard the 74-gun frigate *Captain*. Everywhere were to be seen the scarlet uniforms of King George's most aggressive young generals with crack troops to chase the French from America and put an end to a century of conflict for the western world.

During the past half century, immigrants from continental Europe, Ireland and Scotland had swelled the colonies' population by one-third. Germans, French religious dissenters known as Huguenots and Scotch-Irish, like their English counterparts of the seventeenth century, fled poverty, war and religious persecution for the new, free life in America. The vastness of the land and the limitless opportunity led them to depart from age-old customs and ideas. Soon they shared the new way of life and thought that marked the emerging American.

Artisans and craftsmen swelled the growing towns. Land-hungry farmers, finding the best land along the coast taken up, surged westward into the valley of the Cumberland, down the Shenandoah valley and across the Piedmont plains south to the Carolina back country. The more adventuresome pushed up the Appalachian slopes following the rivers to their fall line.

Sturdy German farmers built prosperous farms in western Pennsylvania, New York, New Jersey and Maryland. Some of the Scotch-Irish pushed farther. They disregarded all rules of settlement and squatted on any spot of vacant ground, preferring to fight off the Indians than to buy up their land titles in an orderly fashion.

" 'Tis against the laws of God and nature that so much land should lie idle," they insisted, "while so many Christians are a' wantin' of it to labor on and raise their bread."

A few brave—or foolhardy—folk spilled over the mountain passes onto the fertile plains that lay beyond. France's savage allies welcomed the intruders with fiery arrows and scalping knives. Few escaped a horrid death or loathsome captivity.

Only eighty thousand Frenchmen were scattered throughout the vast wilderness of New France. But French Jesuits and *voyageurs,* as well as the *coureurs du bois* who hunted and trapped with the Indians, were phenomenally successful in their dealings with the American natives. They lived with the red men on their own terms, respecting their customs and, in turn, commanding the respect and loyalty of the Indian Sachems. Together, the French and the Great Lakes tribes claimed the rich heartland of America.

"English settlements, as they are at present circumscribed," wrote Benjamin Franklin in 1756, "are absolutely at a stand; they are settled up to the mountains."

Born in Boston in 1703, Franklin had kept pace with the growth of his country. He had left Boston as a humble printer's apprentice to make his fortune in the burgeoning city of Philadelphia. By mid-century, Benjamin Franklin was, without doubt, her most eminent citizen and one of the most learned men in all the colonies.

Franklin had made a fortune as publisher of the widely read *Poor Richard's Almanac* and of the *Philadelphia Gazette.* He was, as well, a scientist of world renown with doctorates conferred by Oxford University and St. Andrew's of Scotland. With the learned Professor John Winthrop of Harvard, he shared the rare distinction among colonials of membership in Britain's Royal Philosophical Society. Franklin founded the American Philosophical Society as well as the Library Company and College of Philadelphia.

Somehow Dr. Franklin found time for political activities. In 1754, on the eve of a new war with France, he presented a plan of colonial union under the British crown to representatives of eight colonies. They had met at Albany in June of that year with chiefs of the Six Nations of the Iroquois to frame a treaty of defense. The delegates remained to consider Franklin's farsighted plan of confederation. Approved by the British Lords of Trade who had called the meeting, the plan offered representation in Parliament.

There was widespread propaganda for the union, including the first American editorial cartoon published in Franklin's *Pennsylvania Gazette*. A sick looking snake was depicted, its body severed into eight parts—New England, New York, New Jersey, Pennsylvania, Maryland, Virginia and the Carolinas. The caption warned: "JOIN OR DIE."

Despite imminent danger, the colonial assemblies remained too aware of their rivalries and too greedy of their sovereign rights to give one jot for union, even in their own defense. The Albany Plan was rejected.

"Every Body cries, a Union is absolutely necessary," chided Dr. Franklin. "But when they come to the Manner and Form of the Union, their weak Noddles are perfectly distracted. So if ever there be an Union, it must be form'd at home by the Ministry and Parliament."

Two months later, Great Britain was in a global war with the French. Things went badly in the colonies at first. British commanders had no authority to raise troops or money in a colony without the consent of its assembly. The assemblies voted to raise militia and money only when their own borders were threatened.

Even while howling savages, fortified with French brandy and armed with French muskets, laid waste the frontier towns and massacred British troops sent to protect the settlers, merchants in port cities along the Atlantic coast were carrying on a brisk trade with the French in Canada and the West Indies.

Prime Minister William Pitt moved vigorously to stop this leakage of supplies and to collect duties on foreign goods. In a circular letter to the Royal Governors on August 23, 1760, he exhorted them to apprehend the smugglers whose activities were aiding the enemy.

"Take every step, authorized by law, to bring all such heinous offenders to Punishment."

Colonials had always accepted British regulation of their trade, since the laws that insured profits and goods to the motherland usually fostered their own economies. The Molasses Act of 1733 was an exception, as it sought to cut off a profitable trade with the French Sugar Islands. Shipmasters from Pemaquid, Maine, to Charles Town, South Carolina, ignored its restrictions while Royal Governors and customs officials in the colonies winked at the illegal trade practices. French wines and tropical fruits graced many official tables.

Armed with writs of assistance, royal customs officials began pulling in illegal cargoes on a large scale. The writs were general search warrants authorizing the customs men to be accompanied by a court officer when searching for smuggled goods. The court officer could demand entrance to any suspected ship, shop or warehouse. At the same time, his presence was a safeguard against abuse of power by the customs official. The procedure was common in England.

Writs had been granted in the colonies as well, without complaint.

A writ of assistance, once issued, remained valid during the lifetime of the reigning king. On October 25, 1760, six weeks after his victorious armies took Quebec, King George II died, and his grandson assumed the throne as George III.

In November, 1760, Mr. Cockle, officer of the custom house at Salem, Massachusetts, petitioned the justices of the Superior Court to grant him a "writ of assistants." Chief Justice Stephan Sewall questioned the legality of the writ, and the case was continued until the February term, 1761.

The merchants of the Bay Colony were already feeling the pinch of wartime recession. Each captured cargo increased their anguish. Sixty-three shipowners banded together to try to block further issuance of writs. They engaged the services of two young and brilliant lawyers, James Otis and Oxenbridge Thatcher, to plead their cause.

Before the hearing, Judge Sewall dropped dead. Colonel James Otis of Barnstable, father of young lawyer James, was in line to replace Sewall. He could be expected to protect the interests of the colonial merchants as had Sewall. But the new Royal Governor, Sir Francis Bernard, was a career administrator, eager for advancement. Determined that the Prime Minister's instructions to clamp down on smugglers be carried out, he appointed Lieutenant-Governor Thomas Hutchinson to the judgeship.

By February 24, when the case was to be heard, the whole colony knew that a battle was in store. The council chamber of the Boston Town House on King Street was already filling up when John Adams and his cousin Samuel Quincy pushed their way in to the lawyers' table.

"Good thing we rode up from Braintree last evening!" whispered Samuel. "Looks like every barrister in Middlesex County is here!"

The Flame Is Lit

The protesting merchants sat stiffly at the front of the chamber. Gouty, red-faced Thomas Hancock seemed to dominate the group as he dominated the financial life of Boston. Rumors whispered that his ships did little smuggling. He held contracts for provisioning the king's armies in America, so he remained New England's wealthiest merchant without resorting to illicit trade. He supported his fellow shipmasters on principle, though it meant risking the loss of the valuable royal contracts.

"But where's John?" young Quincy asked John Adams.

As boys, they had played with John Hancock in Braintree. The son of Reverend John Hancock, pastor of the Congregational Church where John Adams' father served as deacon, he had been a thin, shy lad. When Pastor Hancock died, young John, then seven, went to live with his Uncle Thomas and Aunt Lydia in their mansion on Beacon Hill. He became heir apparent to the second largest fortune in the colonies. Meeting him again at Harvard, John Adams had found Hancock quite a dandy, more interested in the ladies and his wardrobe than in his studies. But even the puritanical Adams had to admit that John Hancock was fast becoming as shrewd and dedicated a businessman as his uncle.

"John's been in London these eight months," Adams told Sam Quincy acidly. "I hear he's been presented at court!"

The judges, in their scarlet robes and powdered wigs, were filing in. John Adams took out his notebook and prepared to record the proceedings.

It was two o'clock in the afternoon when James Otis rose to speak. The advocate for the crown and Oxenbridge Thatcher for the merchants had been heard. But it was Otis the crowd awaited.

James Otis was, at 36, one of the most brilliant lawyers in the colony, a student of the classics as well as of the modern political philosophers and scientists. He was a big man, and an unruly shock of black hair was hidden beneath his barrister's wig. Still there was a violence about him, a magnetism that was almost frightening. With his head thrust forward, he began to walk up and down in front of the judges. Adams was certain that Otis was about to do or say something monstrous.

"Your Honors," Otis began quietly, "I will admit that writs of one kind may be legal; that is, special writs, directed to special officers and to search certain houses. But . . . the writ prayed for in this petition, being general, is illegal."

James Otis' voice crackled through the house as he ticked off the ways in which the writs violated men's rights.

"Everyone with this writ may be a tyrant . . . secure in his petty tyranny and spread terror and desolation around him . . . , may enter all houses, shops, etc., at will. . . .

"What a scene does this open! Every man, prompted by revenge, ill humor or wantonness to inspect the inside of his neighbor's house, may get a writ of assistance. . . .

"Now one of the most essential branches of English liberty is the freedom of one's house. A man's house is his castle; and while he is quiet, he is as well guarded as a prince. . . . This writ would totally annihilate this privilege. . . .

"No acts of Parliament can establish such a writ. . . . An act against the constitution is void; an act against natural equity is void. . . ."

On and on Otis talked, but Adams knew that he had stated the heart of his case. The founders of New England had based their charter rights on "natural equity"—the inherent rights of man that had their source in the laws of God and nature.

During the seventeenth century, Sir Isaac Newton had discovered, through his study of nature, that God's universe was indeed ordered by immutable laws, a fact theologians had always assumed. Newton's concept of a "clockwork" universe became widely popular. Soon political philosophers, like Newton's physician friend John Locke, were applying the idea of natural law to the affairs of men.

Man was born free, Dr. Locke maintained, with certain "rights" to life, liberty and property. Men could band together to protect these rights, Locke's "enlightened" theory stated. They had the right to choose their own rulers, and to replace them.

For centuries kings and emperors had ruled by so-called Divine Right. To question it was to invite the rack or the gallows. Yet during the seventeenth century, Englishmen had beheaded one Stuart king and banished another for ruling despotically.

In New England, government by covenant, or agreement, was as old as the Mayflower compact. Each early New England town had been founded by a congregation of Puritans, a covenanted group whose life centered around their church and whose laws were based on Biblical law. Congregational ministers had thundered about the rights of men for half a century. John Adams remembered still how the Reverend John Hancock constantly reminded his congregation in Braintree:

"Our invaluable Massachusetts charter secures to us all the English liberties, besides some additional privileges which the common people in England have not!"

James Otis had now taken those ideas out of the realm of theory and theology . . . Bond servants have rights . . . Black people have rights . . . The last had caused a stir! John Adams shivered as he rode across Boston "Neck" to the mainland in the freezing dampness of that February evening. If a man were subject to no law but that written on his heart, what consequences might result! The young lawyer was certain he would not forget James Otis' speech to his dying day.

"Otis was a flame of fire," Adams was to recall fifty years later. "He hurried away all before him. Every man of an immense audience appeared to me to go away, as I did, ready to take arms against Writs of Assistance. Then and there, was the first scene of the first act of opposition to the arbitrary claims of Great Britain. Then and there, the child Independence was born."

II
TWOPENNY TREASON

*"He has refused his assent to laws . . .
wholesome and necessary for
the public good."*

INDEPENDENCE had not been dreamed of in the Atlantic colonies in the early 1760s. Great Britain rode the high tide of empire, and most of the colonists were loyal sons of Britain. Benjamin Franklin, in London as agent for Pennsylvania, voiced the sentiments of all British Americans:

"No one can more sincerely rejoice than I do on the reduction of Canada; and this is not merely as I am a colonist, but as a Briton."

High hopes were held for the new king. Third of the German princes of the House of Hanover to sit on the throne of Britain, the twenty-two-year-old monarch was the first of his line to speak English without an accent. Born and educated in England, he "gloried" in the name of Briton.

"His Majesty's reign will be happy and truly glorious," predicted Dr. Franklin, who knew the handsome young man personally.

George William Frederick, Elector of Hanover and Monarch of Britain, was industrious and frugal, strictly moral in his personal life and deeply in earnest about his royal vocation. He undoubtedly had the sincerest intentions of making his people happy and prosperous.

George III had been drilled since childhood in the art of being a king. No detail of his kingdom was too small for his attention. "An absolute king must rule absolutely" was the golden rule taught George by his mother and the succession of tutors she hired for him.

Fortunately for George, his capacity for hard work was seemingly inexhaustible. By February, 1763, when the Peace of Paris spelled finis to the Seven Years' War, his kingdom stretched from India to the West Indies and north almost to the Arctic Circle.

British North America alone extended 1,600 miles along the Atlantic seaboard, from Newfoundland to the Florida Keys and west to the Mississippi. Elder mercantilists such as William Pitt believed that the rich French Sugar Islands would have been a more profitable acquisition than the barren wilderness beyond the Alleghenies and the northern fastnesses of Canada. But Pitt seldom agreed with the determined young king. The "Great Commoner," beloved by the people of England and her colonies, was forced to resign his premiership in 1761.

With Pitt went the easygoing imperialism that opposed "novel or harsh measures likely to dampen colonial goodwill and thus injure British trade." The mercantile system had served to govern early scattered trading posts along the Atlantic Coast. But by now the colonies had become thriving states with bustling ports. By the terms of the Peace of Paris, Britain acquired France's enormous inland empire as well. To King George's precise and businesslike mind it seemed essential that the reins of government be tightened so that he could control the diverse peoples and untapped wealth of his American colonies.

Long before French power in continental America was ended, colonial fur trappers, land speculators and settlers greedily eyed the western lands, while the Indians fought any attempt to trespass on their traditional hunting grounds. News that the Great White Father, Louis XVI, meant to cede their land to the British rumbled through the forest like a thunderclap. Traders who understood the Indians warned that the Senecas, Delawares and Shawnees talked of war. They had found a leader in the shrewd Ottawa chief named Pontiac.

Rumblings of the impending trouble seeped back to the Board of Trade in London. Its president, the intelligent and well-informed Earl of Shelburne, suggested a plan to protect the Indians in their hunting grounds. Since there was no immediate need for inland settlements, the Board agreed that the western lands should be kept outside the colonies for the time being. A line running along the crest of the Appalachian Mountains from the St. Lawrence River to the Gulf of Mexico was to be patrolled by British soldiers. The settlers would be kept out, the Indians kept in.

But the wheels of government ground slowly while news took months to cross the Atlantic. Before George III could sign the Proclamation of 1763, the Western tribes were on the warpath.

By mid-June, Pontiac's warriors had overrun most of the British garrisons west of Pittsburgh. Forts Detroit, Pitt and Niagara were under siege. Settlers from the nearby countryside huddled within their walls. Work parties tended nearby fields and orchards under the watchful eye of the British troops.

The Indians harrassed the frontier settlements throughout the summer, plundering and murdering. In the Conococheague Valley of Pennsylvania, every man walked with a cocked musket. Yet he was no match for the stealthy painted savages. Women were murdered as they tended their kitchen gardens, and the heads of children were dashed against the whitewashed cabin walls. The lonely farmer who ran from his plow to save his family invited a slow and horrible death by torture.

Refugees from west of the mountains poured through the passes to camp around villages such as Carlisle in Pennsylvania and Frederick Town in Maryland. George Washington, a young colonel with the Virginia militia, wrote an account of the situation near Frederick for the *Annapolis Gazette:*

> Every day has offered the melancholy scene of poor distressed families driving downwards through this town with their effects, who have deserted their plantations, for fear of falling into the cruel hands of our savage enemies, now daily in the woods.
> We were so sensible of the importance of the Conococheague settlement, that on repeated notice of their growing distress, Captain Butler called the Town Company together, who appeared under arms on the court-house green. . . .

Colonel Washington knew well the "infernal fury" of the "bloodthirsty barbarians." He was not surprised when the twenty men sent from Frederick "to guard the reapers in the lower Conococheague valley, in two days marched back again."

Up and down the frontier, men made the desperate decision to fight. Settlers who braved the wilderness expected no aid from the safe and settled easterners, let alone the faraway government in London.

The Indian rebellion continued into October, when word arrived that the Treaty of Paris had been signed. French officers remaining around Mobile and New Orleans told Pontiac that King Louis would want him to make peace too.

"The word which my father has sent me to make peace I have accepted," Pontiac sadly admitted. "All my young men have buried their hatchets."

Across the sea in London, on October 7 King George

signed the edict calculated to protect the Indians in their hunting grounds and the new lands for "orderly settlement." Canada and East and West Florida were created crown colonies. Their inhabitants were to have all the rights of Englishmen. The whole area between the Appalachians and the Mississippi was reserved to the Indians, for the present.

Although this Proclamation Line violated the vested interests of the colonies, every colonial assembly quickly approved the edict. The great land companies and fur traders reasoned that the exclusion of settlers would work to their advantage.

The Proclamation Line appeared to settle the explosive frontier situation. But new problems arose from it that were to prove insoluble.

The Board of Trade had to decide how to apportion the uncharted land beyond the Alleghenies, and how to support the considerable military force needed along the dividing line for "the security of the settlers."

"In what mode least burdensome and most palatable to the colonies can they contribute to the support?"

The Board of Trade never solved that problem. The new Prime Minister, George Grenville, added it to the mountain of dilemmas he faced in America.

When George Grenville, Pitt's brother-in-law, became Prime Minister in the spring of 1763, he found himself head of a government deep in debt and committed to more responsibility than ever before. England's prewar budget of six and one-half million pounds had rocketed to fourteen and one-half million pounds. English squires and businessmen and West Indian plantation owners bore the burden of taxes. They were also the most powerful group in the House of Commons, where they clamored constantly for relief. To the economy-minded Grenville, the situation appeared intolerable.

A 23-year-old Virginia lawyer named Patrick Henry chose this moment to challenge the right of the king's privy council to "disallow" a law passed by a colonial assembly.

Each colony had been granted in its charter a measure of self-government through its elected assembly. The privy council could make laws for a colony, but in a century and a half of "salutary neglect," few bills concerning the colonies had been sent to Parliament other than trade bills.

Each colony's Royal Governor and council, as well as the king and his council, had the right to "disallow" a law passed by a colonial assembly, especially if they found it inconsistent with English common law. But colonial governors served two masters: those at home, who gave them their commissions, and those in the colonial assembly, who paid their salaries. The hands that hold the purse string hold the power. Neither king nor governors found reason to "disallow" many colonial laws.

During the war, the ancient and loyal colony of Virginia had contributed more than others to its own defense. To do so, the Virginia House of Burgesses had provided for the issuing of bills of credit that were to pass as legal tender, though the act violated the British law forbidding the making of money in the colonies.

The bills of credit were based on tobacco, the principal crop throughout the Chesapeake area, whose value was fairly stable. With tobacco the southern planter met his debts, bought land and paid his taxes.

In 1758, a severe drought brought poor times to Virginia. The tobacco crop was so small that its price shot up. To stabilize its value as currency, the House of Burgesses fixed the value of tobacco at twopence per pound. When the postwar depression worsened the situation, taxpayers were given the choice of paying their tax in tobacco or in local currency.

Twopenny Treason

The act of 1762 "for the Relief of Insolvent Debtors" affected all sides of Virginia life, but proved a particular hardship on the Church of England clergy. As in England, the Anglican church was the official church of Virginia. Its clergy was paid out of taxes at a fixed rate of 17,280 pounds of tobacco a year. Now, with tobacco selling at sixpence per pound, the clergy was being paid in local bills of credit, worth twopence per pound in tobacco. The salary cut in terms of pounds sterling was disastrous, from £400 to £140 (or $2000 to $700). The pittance received by some clergymen for teaching plantation children and slaves did nothing to help the situation. They simply could not feed and clothe their families or pay their debts.

Several ministers, led by the Reverend John Cam, Professor of Divinity at William and Mary College, brought their desperate financial plight to the attention of the Bishop of London, who plead their cause before the British Board of Trade. The result was the disallowance of Virginia's Two Penny Act as contrary to the operation of a royal act forbidding the use of local bills of credit to pay debts. Immediately a number of ministers brought suit to collect back pay from their vestries.

The most famous case was that of the Reverend James Maury, pastor of Fredericksville Parish in Hanover County. In Virginia, as in England, many farmers, artisans and tradesmen of the "middling" sort resented the idea of an established church, lumping its clergy together with the high-living, hard-drinking gentry, kept in luxury by the sweat of the laborers. Dissenters considered it an invasion of their religious liberty to pay taxes to maintain the Anglican clergy.

James Maury was an earnest, hardworking pastor. Of Huguenot descent, he was a classical scholar with liberal political views. Most of the boys in the county had attended his school; some, like Thomas Jefferson had boarded in his home before entering the College of William and Mary. The small stipend for tutoring had helped Maury over the bad years, but with twelve children the going had been rough for him and his family.

No one doubted that Maury was owed something. But since the court could only decide the amount, the lawyer engaged by the vestry decided the case was not worth his time. Patrick Henry, an inexperienced newcomer to the legal profession, took the case.

Henry was a sharp-faced young man with piercing eyes and a strip of mouth that seldom relaxed in a smile. Born in this frontier county on the Piedmont Plateau, he had failed as a farmer and as a merchant before he took up law. In 1760, after six week's study, Patrick Henry went before the Attorney-General, elegant and learned Peyton Randolph, to be examined for the bar. Randolph later declared to friends that the backwoods lad was "extraordinarily ignorant, even for a lawyer."

"Then why was he granted a license?" wondered Tom Jefferson when he heard the story from Peyton's younger brother John, a fellow law student.

"Because, Peyt says, the man has a kind of genius for talk," John Randolph confided, "and he's promised to learn the law."

Patrick's father, John Henry, was one of three judges to hear the Parson's Cause on December 1, 1763. The gallery of the Hanover County Court House was packed with gentry in velvet breeches and powdered wigs. Twenty Anglican clergymen stared down from the front bench like vengeful white-throated blackbirds.

The jury, Patrick Henry was relieved to note, was made up of twelve plain farmers, four of whom he knew to be dissenters. They would be helpful to his case. The backwoods lawyer meant to seize this opportunity to attack the established church and challenge the king's prerogative as well. He would make a routine case into a *"cause célèbre"* and a name for himself at the same time.

"Mr. Henry . . . harangued the jury for near an hour," the Reverend Mr. Maury recalled. "He labored to prove that the act had every characteristic of a good law . . . that the King, by disallowing Acts of this salutary nature, from being the father of his people, degenerated into a tyrant, and forfeits all rights to his subjects' obedience. . . ."

At this point in the proceedings, Maury's lawyer shouted, "Treason! The man speaks treason!" Trembling with rage, the lawyer turned to the judges, who sat silent, as if bewitched.

"He called the King a tyrant! How can your worships hear him without emotion?"

There was a murmur from the gallery; it was silenced by the Judge's gavel. The presiding justice ordered Henry to continue.

"Who," asked the young lawyer, "is the ruler in the great colony of Virginia? The King—an alien across the sea? Or the Burgesses, representatives of the people of Virginia? If the King is father to his subjects, how can he denounce a law so needful to the welfare of the common man? If a father betray his children they owe him no allegiance!"

The jury, "containing four dissenters" according to Maury's report, "in less than five minutes brought in a verdict for me of one penny damages."

The jury had "found" for the clergyman, as it was bound to according to Virginia law, but in granting him only one penny, they showed where their sympathies lay.

Like James Otis, Patrick Henry had sounded a clear call to all his fellow Americans. The colonists were freeborn Englishmen. They believed in the rule of law to protect their rights and privileges as Englishmen. If a law was not a good law, it must be changed. If a king were not a good king. . . .

Englishmen in the past century had beheaded one king and deposed another to protect their rights, Otis had reminded Americans. Patrick Henry suggested that it could happen again.

III

THE SONS OF LIBERTY

". . . For imposing taxes on us without our Consent . . ."

GEORGE III sat upon the throne of England by the grace of Parliament rather than the grace of God. A century of civil strife had transferred the power of the British government from crown to Parliament.

Most colonists remained fiercely loyal to their sovereign. Few believed Parliament had any power to legislate for them, let alone tax them. This was the sole right of their elected assemblies. It said so right in the charters, and the colonial charters came directly from the king.

The American colonies, in 1763, differed widely one from another, in their way of life, their religion, their social customs. The frontiersman in his log hut, grubbing an existence for his family against tremendous odds, was apt to be quite radical in his ideas compared to seaboard dwellers. Yet one belief was held in common up and down the Atlantic seaboard and west to the Mississippi; the colonial charters were sacred documents assuring to the colonists all the rights of freeborn Englishmen and full protection under British law.

When economy-minded George Grenville took the office of Prime Minister in April, 1763, his first challenge was the national debt, which had risen to a horrifying one hundred and forty-seven million pounds when peace came with the French. He found that Britons were already loaded with taxes. There were stamp duties requiring tax stamps for all legal documents, newspapers, tavern licenses—an endless list that included every piece of paper or parchment, even playing cards. A tax had to be paid on glass for windows, on malt for ale, even on cider. Grenville put into effect new economy measures that reached even into the king's household. Still they were not enough to make up the deficit.

British Americans, on the other hand, at the time enjoyed one of the lowest tax rates of any people in the Western world. Yet much of the debt had been accumulated during the wars in these colonies, while a sizable portion of the British budget was still going to maintain troops there, along the Proclamation Line and for general administrative costs. To the Prime Minister it seemed obvious that the colonists should pay their share of expenses. He proposed that the stamp duties be extended to America. True, Parliament had never imposed a direct tax on the colonies but few in England doubted that it had the power to do so.

The colonists did not agree. Revenue might be raised for the king from customs duties, and they could only grumble.

"But," colonial agents warned the Prime Minister, "they may do more than grumble if you attempt to raise a revenue to pay the costs of royal government or the salary of royal troops."

Jared Ingersoll, agent for New York, showed Mr. Grenville the passage in his colony's Charter of Liberties and Privileges relating to taxation:

> That Noe aid, Tax, Tallage, Assessment, Custome, Loane, Benevolence or Imposition whatsoever shall be layed assessed imposed or levyed on any of his Majestyes Subjects within this province or their Estates upon any manner of Colour or pretence but by the act and Consent of the Governour Councell and Representatives of the People in Generall Assembly mett and Assembled.

The Prime Minister found the distinction between external taxes, or duties, and internal or direct taxes as absurd as it was irritating.

"What a pother!" he complained, "whether the money is to be taken out of their coat pocket or out of their waistcoat pocket! British soldiers fighting to protect your frontiers have not been paid in months!" Grenville pointed out. "Yet some of your wealthy New York Patroons have incomes from estates on the Hudson that are as large as an English shire. A revenue must be raised in America to meet the cost of government and defense."

The Treasury Board had already drafted a bill to extend stamp duties to the colonies. On advice of the colonial agents, Grenville held it back in favor of further customs duties, which he requested of Parliament in March, 1764.

But he told the agents, "if the colonial assemblies cannot come up with a plan to raise an 'adequate' or 'equivalent' sum, stamp duties must be levied in the colonies."

Boston was a ghost town that winter of 1764. In January, an epidemic of smallpox sent families scurrying to the country. Merchants who had survived the depression carried their stock to nearby villages and set up shop in private homes. Governor Bernard and his council, along with the House of Representatives, fled to Cambridge, across the Charles River, where they established temporary quarters in Harvard Hall and the college's newly built Hollis Hall.

Thomas Hancock, a member of the Governor's council, packed his wife Lydia and nephew John into the family coach, to follow the crowd across the Neck, Boston's one link with the mainland. A retinue of household servants followed with their considerable baggage. Besides his government contracts to supply His Majesty's troops in America, Thomas Hancock had cornered the lucrative whale oil market. He remained one of the richest men in the province. His rage over the writs of assistance had been short-lived.

"This depression is widespread," puffed Uncle Thomas, "and not caused by any British restrictions on our trade."

Nephew John, then 27, was not convinced. He had joined the Masonic Lodge of St. Andrew's where he met outspoken critics of Parliament like the 26-year-old goldsmith and engraver Paul Revere, and the eloquent young Dr. Joseph Warren. With them he visited the loft over the shop where the *Boston Gazette* was printed. The tall, handsome merchant in his impeccable London attire seemed out of place in the long, crowded room, which had a ceiling so low his powdered wig brushed the rafters. There John Hancock was surprised to find his quiet country schoolmate John Adams hobnobbing with avowed enemies of the Royal government, one of whom was James Otis. Otis' special target was Lieutenant-Governor Thomas Hutchinson, who had been named Chief Justice over his father.

"Hutchinson may be a Massachusetts man," Otis maintained, "but he's hand in glove with his Royal Nibs, Bernard. Besides, he's got all his relatives, and his wife's relatives, into the seats of government. There's no way to beat such power but to set the province in flames!"

All the young members of the "Long Room" club chafed at some aspects of British rule, but few would have countenanced open rebellion, not even their eldest and most controversial member, Samuel Adams.

Samuel Adams, at 42, appeared to be a born loser. He seemed unable either to make or to keep money. Every business enterprise he attempted ended in failure. Certainly he looked a failure in his worn untidy clothes and unkempt wig that always sat askew. He had lost his wife and three of his five children—but he numbered his friends in the thousands.

Sam Adams had never left the provincial capital except to attend Harvard. There his study of political philosophers, Locke among others, had confirmed his devotion to liberty and the colony's charter rights instilled in him by his father, Deacon Adams.

Politics became Sam Adams' religion, and he preached his beliefs with all the zeal of his Puritan forebears. His endeavor leaped social barriers. Dockworker or shipowner, marketman and merchant—he knew them all. He was a member of all three of Boston's Caucus clubs that met before each Town Meeting to decide what stand to take on every issue and what candidates to put up for every office. Restlessly he toured the town's numerous taverns, from the Salutation in the North End to the Royal Exchange in Market Square. No shade of political opinion escaped him.

Yet even as a politician he seemed a failure. He had held a number of minor jobs, including that of tax collector. As a collector he was always short in his accounts. So many people had been thrown out of work by the depression, so many were hungry and wanting the barest necessities, that Sam Adams could never bring himself to press them for back taxes.

By spring of 1764, trade in Boston—indeed, throughout the colonies—had nearly ground to a halt. That May, news arrived that Parliament had passed a new revenue bill, called the Sugar Act.

Colonial assemblies had been warned by their agents to expect new duties. None objected to the principle of the Sugar Act. Dr. Franklin, just returned from London, declared himself "not much alarm'd about your schemes for raising money on us." But, after reading the bill, every colony filed a protest.

The Sugar Act sailed under false colors. Its provisions were quite different from what the name implied. While actually reducing the duty on sugar and molasses, new restrictions were introduced on big exports like hides and logwood, and new duties were placed on popular imports, such as French fabrics and Madeira wine.

But the alarm bell rang in almost hidden provisions. The British Navy was authorized to patrol American waters in search of smugglers. The jurisdiction of the vice-admiralty courts was extended so certain common law cases might be tried without benefit of jury.

The most irritating provision of the "Black Act," as it came to be called, was the extension of British duties to intercolonial trade. A shipper was required to post bond even if he traveled no farther than from Jersey across the Hudson River to New York.

The whole was topped off with a warning that a "charge of certain stamp duties in the plantations" would follow unless colonial assemblies could devise a better way to provide for their own government and protection.

Boston's reaction was prompt and violent. Hitherto conservative merchants lent dignity to a noisy town meeting where James Otis presented his statement of "The Rights of the British Colonies," later published in pamphlet form. His arguments were an extension of those against the writs of assistance—"with the additional point," recorded John Adams, "that taxation without representation was unconstitutional and therefore ... such taxes [are] void."

"One single act of Parliament has set the people thinking more than in their whole lives before," Otis declared, calling for a special session of the legislature. "We must set about taxing ourselves, or at least prevent Parliament's tax."

John Adams noted casually an innovation introduced at that town meeting which was to snowball into disaster for British colonial aspirations in America.

"A committee was appointed to correspond with patriots

in other colonies," he wrote, "and plans were laid for a campaign to bring economic pressure to bear on the Mother Country."

The New York legislature declared that exemption from parliamentary taxation was a "Right" without which "there can be No Liberty, No Happiness, No Security." At the same time, the wealthy merchants of that colony joined with those of Boston to urge "the absolute necessity" of cutting down imports from Britain by turning to manufacturing. They flouted England's oldest restrictions on the colonies by entering into associations to make woolens and other items normally bought in England.

"They have set a number of hands to spinning," Jared Ingersoll reported, "have erected distilleries to make corn spirits instead of molasses-based rum, and are planning ways of increasing the stock of sheep."

Cutting down the consumption of lamb and mutton was the chief means of accomplishing the latter. Meanwhile college students rallied to the cause by depriving themselves in other areas.

"The young gentlemen of Yale College," announced the *New York Gazette* of November 22, 1764, "have unanimously agreed not to make use of any foreign spiritous liquors. . . . All Gentlemen of Taste . . . think themselves better entertained with a good Glass of Beer or Cider than with the best Madeira."

The Irish settlers of Pennsylvania raised flax as they had at home and made very good linens, while a thread-stocking industry in Germantown was already booming.

Peaceful Quakers were more disturbed by the Mutiny and Quartering Act, passed at the same time as the Sugar Act, which specified that additional troops would be sent to America and housed in public inns and barns. John Dickinson, a conservative Philadelphia lawyer, pointed out in a newspaper article that the British Army had not protected the frontiers during the recent Indian uprising. And why, he asked, were there so few colonial officers?

"Such a formidable force established in the midst of peace," stormed the London-educated barrister, "must be to bleed America into submission!"

Benjamin Franklin customarily opposed Dickinson on domestic issues, but in this matter he was forced to agree. Returning to England as Pennsylvania's agent, he racked his brain for an alternative to the proposed stamp tax.

"The more you charge us to care and pay for troops," he warned the Prime Minister, "the less you will receive from us."

"I am not set upon this tax," Grenville assured him. "But," he reiterated, "we have the power to tax them, and we will."

Franklin, along with several other colonial agents, did offer plans for self-taxation to replace the stamp duties. Colonial representation in Parliament was again suggested.

By the system of "virtual representation," every member of the British Parliament represented, in theory, every district and class in the Empire. Owing to property restrictions, only 160,000 of the 8,000,000 Britons were qualified to vote. Seats were often bought. In Commons as well as in the House of Lords, seats were handed down from father to son like a piece of property. A fox-hunting squire from Surrey, for instance, was supposed to represent not only his own yeomen but artisans from the huge industrial cities of the midlands, miners from Wales and the planters, shipbuilders, merchants and fishermen of the Atlantic colonies in America.

Colonial Englishmen did not believe that one man could represent the interests of so varied a group. Representatives must be "Persons chosen by themselves." Such "actual" representation existed in their own assemblies, and colonists saw no reason to brave the long sea voyage to England, to endure the expense and temptations of London, all for the doubtful privilege of sitting in an assembly where their voices would probably not be heard anyway.

The colonists' pleas of continuing debt due to the French wars roused little sympathy in England, since the British people bore a greater burden. Living conditions in England were even worse than in the colonies, with poor harvests and rising living costs adding to the growing unrest. There were riots in western England over the cider tax. Workers in the silk industry marched on London to demand relief from French competition. Small wonder the ministry and the Lords of Trade all but ignored the yearlong spate of petitions from the colonies.

George Grenville presented his proposal for American stamp duties in his budget message to Parliament on February 6, 1765. He had gone out of his way to sugarcoat the more irritating features of the bill. Certainly it was less rigorous than the stamp tax then in effect in Britain. All stamp agents were to be Americans. All revenue from the stamps would remain in America to meet expenses there, thus preventing a drain of precious specie.

A few members of the House argued against the proposals—

". . . gentlemen interested in the West Indies," reported Jared Ingersoll, who attended the debate, "members connected with some of the colonies, a few heads of the minority, successors to the policies of William Pitt. Sir Isaac Barré gave a very handsome and moving speech."

Sir Isaac Barré was a Huguenot refugee who had become Member of Parliament from Ireland. A soldier turned statesman, he had served many years in the colonies. He had fought beside colonial troops at Quebec and felt a continuing warm regard for Americans. He listened quietly as Charles Townshend, first Lord of Trade, argued strongly in favor of the measures. Townshend's own plan for provincial control was known to be far more rigorous.

"And now," Townshend concluded, "will these Americans, children planted by our care, nourished up by our indulgence until they are grown, protected by our arms, will they grudge to contribute their mite to relieve us from the weight of the burden which we lie under?"

Townshend's words, so typical of British official attitude toward the colonies, were too much for Barré. The bullet scar across his left cheek, a memento of the Quebec siege, was an angry red. He jumped to his feet, shouting:

"They planted by your care? No! Your oppressions planted them in America. They fled from your tyranny. . . . They grew by your neglect. . . . Your care was exercised in sending persons to rule them . . . , to spy out their liberties . . . , to misrepresent their actions, to prey upon them, whose behavior has caused the blood of these Sons of Liberty to recoil within them!"

It was no use. To most members the principle of the stamp tax appeared so logical that they barely noticed the debate. On February 27, 1765, the House of Commons passed the American stamp tax with a vote of 250-50. A week later, on March 8, the Lords passed the bill unanimously.

George Grenville boasted that the burden of the stamp tax would fall with equal weight on all the colonies, and on the western settlements as well as on the merchants and planters of the east. Had the Prime Minister, the Treasury and the Lords of Trade set out to unite the colonies against the British government, they could not have done a more efficient job.

"On and after the First Day of November, one thousand

seven hundred and sixty-five," the bill read, "to be paid to His Majesty, his Heirs and Successors, for every skin or piece of vellum or parchment, or sheet or piece of paper, on which shall be ingrossed, written or printed . . . within the British colonies and plantations, a stamp duty of three-pence. . . . A sterling Halfpenny Stamp on every Half Sheet of a Newspaper, and Two Shillings Sterling on every Advertisement. . . ."

In effect the Stamp Act meant that no hamlet in any colony could carry on its business without the stamped paper. No tavern could operate legally, no game of cards could be played. Even legal wedlock was discouraged by the £2 stamp duty on marriage licenses.

Nor would officers be necessary to enforce the stamp tax, since any document that lacked stamps would be useless. A lawyer or businessman who tried to conduct his business with unstamped paper would be tried in a vice-admiralty court, before a crown-appointed judge and without benefit of jury.

Yet no one in England, including the colonial agents, dreamed that the offensive measures would be resisted. Benjamin Franklin, like the other agents, had labored hard to keep the bill from being passed. Now it was law, practical Ben secured the post of stamp distributor for friends in several colonies. With typical thrift, he ordered a hundred reams of oversized half-sheets for his *Pennsylvania Gazette* in the vain hope of evading the full tax.

"I think the tax will affect the Printers more than anybody," he wrote to his partner.

The Editor-printers of the twenty-three newspapers in the colonies were certain they would be ruined. Pamphlets and almanacs, a large portion of their business, were also subjected to a high tax. Foreign-language presses were assessed double, a verdict of death for Pennsylvania German papers, for instance, which until then had stood aloof from colonial politics.

Newssheets bordered in black reported the Stamp Act provisions.

"They mean to strip us of the means of knowledge!" stormed John Adams in an article written for the *Boston Gazette*.

The colonial press was indeed a source of information. Many editors, like Franklin, were postmasters as well. Through them, news of events sped from one colony to another. Much of their material was reprinted from English and European papers. Newspapers had no tradition as opinion makers, certainly not as defiers of the law. Bewilderment and uncertainty were the first reactions to the stamp tax. Only a few bold spirits attempted to fight the act.

The town of Worcester, Massachusetts, instructed its representatives to the colonial legislature to "take special care of the LIBERTY OF THE PRESS." The *Connecticut Gazette* anounced that a newspaper was "the guardian of freedom." But it was a curious case of misreporting that gave impetus to the agitation over the stamp tax, welded together public opinion and gave leadership and direction to men throughout the colonies.

The trumpet call to action sounded from Virginia, the king's own "Old Dominion." Before a single stamped paper landed on the shores of North America, the "Sons of Liberty" were on the march.

IV

THE TRUMPET SOUNDS

". . . To secure these rights . . ."

THE Crown Colony of Virginia was the oldest and the largest of the Atlantic provinces. By the original charter grant from the king its territory stretched "from the Point of Land called Cape or Point Comfort all along the Sea Coasts to the Northward two hundred miles; . . . to the Southward two hundred Miles; and . . . up into the Land throughout from Sea to Sea West and Northwest. . . ."

Gentlemen adventurers had "planted" the Virginia colony and remained loyal to the Stuart kings even during the period of Puritan rule. When Charles II returned from exile, he fondly dubbed Virginia "My Old Dominion."

Tidewater aristocrats along the coast were proud of their English heritage. Like English squires, they loved hunting and cockfights, good food and fine wines. They were openhanded hosts, welcoming friend and stranger alike, for there were few hostels or inns in the territory.

The "borderers" in the central and western counties were of German descent, or Scotch-Irish like Patrick Henry. Others were descended from English debtors who had come to Virginia as bond servants and then taken up land to the west when their terms of indenture were over. Few of these had reason to feel love or loyalty toward England.

Colonial boundaries meant little to the restless back-country folk. Men moved freely up and down the frontier, where dividing lines became lost in the uncharted wilderness.

A few English gentlemen and independent yeomen penetrated the frontier early, fighting off hostile Indians to take out huge territorial claims on the Piedmont Plateau. Only two white men preceded Peter Jefferson in the upland county of Goochland—Isham and William Randolph, members of one of Virginia's oldest and finest families. In 1739, Peter married Isham's daughter, Jane. Four years later, just before their first son, Thomas Jefferson, was born, the couple moved even farther west to St. James Parish on the Northanna River.

Despite his family's isolation, Tom received a solid, if unorthodox education from a Calvinist preacher, Douglas Scot. Peter Jefferson himself taught his son to read Latin and Greek, while the learned and liberal Huguenot minister, James Maury, prepared young Tom for college. At fifteen, Thomas Jefferson entered the College of William and Mary at Williamsburg.

The planters' capital of Williamsburg was a country town compared to the large colonial ports. Only a thousand inhabitants, black and white, occupied the two hundred simple wooden homes scattered on either side of the principal thoroughfare, the Duke of Gloucester Street. Except for the college, there were only two buildings of any consequence—the palatial governor's mansion and the Capitol, an "airy building" on the square where the general court and legislature met.

During the "Publick Times" when court and assembly were in session, Williamsburg's population doubled. Then broad, tree-lined Duke of Gloucester Street was a lively scene. Ladies from the plantations along the James River came to town, resplendent in their silks and plumes. Robed judges and burgesses in velvet breeches and fancy waistcoats mingled with farmers in buckskin and Indian chiefs with feathered headdresses.

Tom Jefferson loved these gay times. But on this Wednesday morning, May 29, 1765, he found the crowds and carriages irritating obstructions as he sped toward his law professor's home. He took a shortcut across the Palace green into George Wythe's garden through a back gate. The warm morning air was sweet with the scent of flowering crab and boxwood. The balding little lawyer was already in his garden. He looked up surprised at his favorite student, whose usually pallid face was almost as red as his hair.

George Wythe, though not yet forty, was one of the most learned lawyers in the colonies and an influential member of Virginia's House of Burgesses. Wythe, a self-taught man, had initiated the first formal legal training course in North America. Every student at William and Mary clamored to attend his scholarly lectures. Tom Jefferson studied with him during his college years and was now reading for his law degree in Wythe's office.

"It's the Stamp Act, sir," Tom was panting. "Patrick Henry had a copy at the Raleigh Tavern last night. He's in a rage! I think he's prepared some resolutions to present to the House."

"But most of the Burgesses have gone home," exclaimed Wythe. "George Washington left for Mount Vernon only yesterday. All four Lees have gone to superintend the spring planting."

The two men went into the house while Wythe adjusted his wig and gown. The burgess confided to Jefferson: "Governor Fauquier hoped to hold back the terms of the obnoxious act until the fall session."

The Governor's elaborate coach, with its team of six milk-white horses, was already drawn up in front of the Capitol as Jefferson and Wythe pushed their way through the crowds gathered on the square. Many people were reading a SUPPLEMENT EXTRAORDINARY of the *Virginia Gazette*. Editor Will Hunter had his apprentice stationed at the entrance to the House of Burgesses while his two slaves were hawking the half-sheet supplement.

"Was Hunter with Patrick Henry last night?" Wythe asked.

"Indeed he was," Jefferson replied.

"Doubtless he received news of the Stamp Act provisions from editors in the northern colonies," George Wythe surmised. "No wonder Henry's dander is up!" he added as he scanned the special edition he had just bought.

At that moment, Peyton Randolph, Virginia's Attorney-General, sped up in his small gig, threw the reins to a groom, then swept lawyer Wythe into the House chamber with him. Jefferson joined a fellow student, John Tyler, at the entrance just as Speaker John Robinson banged his gavel for order.

Thirty-nine delegates remained out of one hundred and sixteen. Half were clustered around the green baize table in the center of the room, talking excitedly and all at once. Jeweled hands gesticulated wildly, powdered heads bobbed. The nervous snap of silver snuff boxes was clearly audible above the din.

"Gentlemen, please," begged the usually imperturbable speaker. "We must consider immediately what steps are necessary as a consequence of the resolutions of the House of Commons of Great Britain relative to the charging of certain stamp duties in the Colonies and Plantations of America."

Before the burgesses were settled in their seats, George Johnston, delegate from Fairfax, moved that the House go into Committee of the Whole to consider the Stamp Act. Patrick Henry seconded the motion. The two men sat side by side in the third tier of benches. Behind them were eighteen frontier delegates. Silent till now, they gave their "aye" to the motion as one voice.

The clerk put the mace beneath the table as Robinson climbed down from the speaker's dais to give place to the presiding officer, Attorney-General Peyton Randolph. Immediately Patrick Henry was on his feet.

"Sir, I beg to be heard on this mighty issue," Henry began.

Peyton Randolph looked at him with mingled distaste and apprehension. Henry's thin, wiry frame was clad in a dingy black suit beneath his barrister's robe. To Randolph's discerning eye, his stock and ruffled shirt did not seem quite clean. At the same time, Randolph remembered all too well the man's gift for silver-tongued oratory. He had granted Patrick Henry his law license against his better judgment. Now he had no choice but to let him speak.

"The chair recognizes the delegate from Louisa County," Randolph drawled.

Patrick Henry drew a crumpled sheet of paper from his pocket and began to read:

> Whereas, the honorable House of Commons in England have of late drawn into question how far the General Assembly of this Colony hath power to enact laws for laying of taxes and imposing duties . . . the House of Burgesses have come to the following resolves:
> That the first adventurers and settlers of this his Majesty's colony and dominion brought with them and transmitted to their posterity . . . all the privileges . . . possessed by the people of Great Britain.

So far there was no argument. The House listened in tense silence until Henry reached the fifth resolve.

> That the taxation of the people [should be] by themselves, or by persons chosen by themselves to rep-

resent them, who can only know what taxes the people are able to bear . . . and are equally affected by such taxes themselves. . . .

Patrick Henry paused and glanced around the chamber. His dark eyes flashed. Then he thundered:

Resolved, therefore, that the General Assembly of this colony have the *only* and *exclusive* right and power to lay taxes and impositions upon the inhabitants of this colony, and that every attempt to vest such power in any person or persons whatsoever . . . has a manifest tendency to destroy British as well as American freedom!

Henry's words crackled across the silent room like lightning across a still but ominous sky. George Wythe and Peyton Randolph, the most knowledgeable lawyers present, realized at once the treasonable implication that this act of Britain's Parliament need not—nay, *should not*—be obeyed! Before either could protest, Patrick Henry shouted: "Tarquin and Caesar had each his Brutus, Charles the First his Cromwell, and George the Third . . ."

There was a stir amongst the powdered heads. Randolph and George Wythe were on their feet crying "Treason!"

"Treason! Treason!" echoed from the floor.

"And George the Third," repeated Patrick Henry, seeming to grow taller as he drew himself up to hurl his parting barb. "George III may profit by their example! If *this* be treason, make the most of it."

Suddenly the House of Burgesses broke into unbridled frenzy. Every member was on his feet.

"Henry speaks as Homer wrote!" Thomas Jefferson whispered excitedly to his companion.

John Tyler was spellbound by the scene. "It seems like a warning flash from history," he declared.

The two student lawyers stood in the doorway through-

The Trumpet Sounds

out the daylong debate. That evening, Jefferson recorded his recollection of the proceedings.

> Mr. Henry moved and Mr. Johnston seconded these resolutions successively. They were opposed by Messrs. Randolph, Bland, Pendleton, Wythe, and all the old members whose influence in the House had, till then, been unbroken.

Jefferson was in the Capitol lobby the next morning long before the House bell rang.

Colonel Peter Randolph, a member of Governor Fauquier's council, was sitting at the clerk's table thumbing through the House journals.

"When I was clerk," the councilman told his young kinsman, "a vote of the House was expunged. I cannot recall which one. I'm seeking the record."

Evidently the precedent was found, for on May 30, the vote on Henry's "treasonable" fifth resolution was erased from the journal. Governor Fauquier, relieved of the necessity of sending the offending resolution to the Lords of Trade in London, dissolved the House of Burgesses on June 1, 1765.

Henry had tucked two more resolutions back in his pocket. On June 24, the *Newport Mercury* published all seven "Virginia Resolves" as if they had been voted upon by the Virginia Assembly. The last two were an open invitation to rebellion.

> ... The inhabitants of this colony *are not bound to yield obedience* to any law ... other than the laws of the General Assembly aforesaid [Virginia's Burgesses].
> Any Person who shall ... assert or maintain ... that Persons other than the General Assembly of this Colony have any right or Power to lay any taxation on the people here, shall be deemed an enemy to this his Majesty's colony.

The Virginia resolves were accepted throughout the colonies as the voice of America's most powerful colony. In Philadelphia and New York they were whispered about privately, "being accounted treasonable," but newspapers throughout New England copied them as printed in the *Newport Mercury*.

"This is treason!" exclaimed James Otis when he read them in the *Boston Gazette*. But Oxenbridge Thatcher, the lawyer who had plead with Otis against the writs of assistance, exulted from his deathbed:

"Oh, they are men! They are noble spirits!"

Massachusetts had reacted with surprising calmness to the Stamp Act. When the Assembly met in June, James Otis suggested that a circular letter be sent to all the colonies inviting them to participate in a general congress. Their elected representatives would meet in New York City on the first Tuesday of October "to consider a general and united, dutiful and humble representation of their condition to his Majesty and the Parliament, to implore relief."

Reaction to the suggestion was slow. The last intercolonial congress at Albany had accomplished little. Never had such a meeting been held except by order of the Lords of Trade.

During the summer of 1765, the rebellious spirit of Patrick Henry's resolutions infected people up and down the Atlantic seaboard. Secret organizations calling themselves the Sons of Liberty sprang up in every colony. They took Henry's last resolution very seriously and meant to punish "enemies" of the colony themselves. Their first target was the men elected as stamp distributors.

Boston awoke on the morning of August 14 to find an effigy of Andrew Oliver, the stamp officer appointee, hanging from a huge elm tree at the corner of Newbury and Elm Streets. Every effort to cut down the dummy was prevented by the crowd of dockworkers, marketmen and out-of-work sailors that grew throughout the afternoon.

"The leaders are not there, mark you," Governor Bernard told his council when they met together at the Town House to plan a counterattack. "They may be solid citizens of the town. Businessmen, artisans . . ."

"And newspaper editors," added his Lieutenant-Governor, Thomas Hutchinson, Oliver's brother-in-law.

"Probably that rascal Sam Adams," someone else suggested. "He writes regularly for that weekly dung-barge, *The Gazette!*"

The mob was marching toward the Town House, chanting "Liberty and Property! No Stamps." They carried poor Oliver's facsimile up Beacon Hill to his home, where they chopped off its head. Later they burned it in a huge bonfire, while the original watched from his window horrified.

"You and the Governor had best go out to Castle William in the harbor," Hutchinson told his brother-in-law. "The Navy ships can protect you there."

When Hutchinson, Chief Justice Story and the Sheriff tried to reason with the mob's ringleaders, they were met by a volley of stones. Later in the month their houses, along with Oliver's, were all but demolished, the manuscript of Hutchinson's painstaking history of Massachusetts Bay trampled in the mud.

With the same mindless violence, riots flared throughout the summer in Newport and New York and in cities down the coast. They went far beyond anything opposition leaders could condone. Sam Adams called them "high-handed outrages" while merchants like John Hancock bombarded business associates in England with letters spelling out the consequences if the stamp tax went into effect.

"You will find it come to pass that the people of this Country will never suffer themselves to be made slaves of," wrote Hancock. "I am determined as soon as I know that they insist on the act, to Sell my Stock & Shut up my Warehouse Doors. Thus much I told our Govr. . . .

"I have a Right to the Libertys & Privileges of the English Constitution," Hancock added, "& I as an Englishman will enjoy them."

On the eve of the Stamp Act Congress, Benjamin Franklin's cartoon of the divided snake, used originally against the French, was published in some New York and Jersey papers. With the same slogan "Join or Die," it was now directed against Britain.

As before, nine colonies sent delegates to the Congress. New Hampshire and Georgia sent notes expressing their sympathy with the objectives, but never got around to electing representatives. Governor Fauquier of Virginia, anxious to avoid more trouble, simply refused to call a special session of the legislature to elect delegates.

The Stamp Act Congress met in New York on October 7 in an atmosphere of uneasy calm. New York's Governor Colden called the meeting "unconstitutional, unprecedented and unlawful." The Board of Trade in London considered the gathering of colonial delegates without its sanction a "dangerous precedent."

The Congress tried to put resistance back on a dignified level. Its "Declaration of Rights and Grievances" was judicious and precise. Vowing allegiance to the crown and "all due Subordination to that August Body the Parliament of Great Britain," the document stated:

> That it is . . . the undoubted right of *Englishmen,* that no Taxes be imposed on them, but with their Consent, given personally, or by their Representatives.
> That the only Representatives . . . are Persons chosen by themselves. . . .
> That the late Act of Parliament, entitled, *An Act*

for granting and applying certain Stamp Duties . . . and several other acts, extending the Jurisdiction of the Courts of Admiralty beyond its ancient Limits, have a manifest Tendency to subvert the Rights and Liberties of the Colonists.

That it is the indispensable Duty of these Colonies, to the best of Sovereigns, to the Mother Country . . . to endeavor . . . to procure the Repeal of the Act. . . .

A child might have governed so loyal a people. Even a stubborn, willful sovereign like George might have kept those "brightest jewels" secure in his crown. All the constitutional reasons for their rebellion had been stated. He had only to follow the simple rules laid down by his subjects overseas. There is no indication that he ever read their petitions.

The time seemed already too late for judicious petitions to a sovereign who appeared to be deaf. The spirit of rebellion was in the streets if not in the legislatures of the land.

"There ought to be no New England man, no New Yorker, known on the continent," Christopher Gadsden of South Carolina had told the Stamp Act Congress, "but all of us Americans."

For the first time, nine of the twelve colonies had acted together. The proceedings of their Congress were approved by the rest. The colonies had taken a giant step, away from Britain toward union.

V

REBELLION POSTPONED

> "... Governments are instituted ...,
> deriving their just powers from the
> consent of the governed ..."

GEORGE III regretted almost from the beginning his choice of George Grenville as Lord Privy Seal. The dour little Prime Minister bored the young monarch with constant lectures on the need for stricter economies. Besides, the appointment had stirred up a political hornets' nest.

The extreme Whig MP, John Wilkes, had voiced such violent opposition to Grenville in issue #45 of a paper called *The North Briton* that he had been imprisoned in the Tower of London charged with treason. Because of his parliamentary immunity, Wilkes could not be held for trial. Released, he fled to the continent, but not before his name and the number "45" became a rallying cry for liberty-loving Whigs throughout the Empire.

The last straw for the young king was the bill Grenville pushed through Parliament that "excluded the king's mother from the government in case the king should be incapacitated by ill health."

King George was often ill, with frequent colds and pleurisy, aggravated by England's damp climate. Some whispered he was touched with madness when unbearable headaches kept him confined for days in a darkened room. Whatever the cause, the king's ministers agreed that a board of regency should be set up in case serious indisposition should interfere with his monarchical duties.

When George discovered that Prime Minister Grenville had succeeded in barring the Dowager Princess of Wales from the Regency Board, he flew into a rage. In May, 1765, long before anyone in England dreamed that his stamp tax would be resisted in the colonies, George Grenville was thrown out of office.

Grenville was replaced by Charles Wentworth-Watson, First Marquess of Rockingham, a rather petulant young man, but as warmhearted and broadminded as his predecessor had been cold and calculating. A political novice, Rockingham formed a ministry of old government hands, men inclined to Pitt's Whiggish hands-off attitude toward the colonies. Only the "Great Commoner," William Pitt, aging and crippled with gout, refused Rockingham's plea to come out of retirement at Bath. Not until news of the fierce colonial resistance to the stamp tax drifted back across the Atlantic did the beloved statesman publicly declare his support of the American position.

All through the summer and autumn of 1765, British headlines screamed of riots in the colonies. There were warnings of the ruin of the British economy because of the American boycott. Angry articles spewed forth from both sides of the Atlantic, some denouncing, some supporting the tax with equal passion.

Colonial pulpits, in addition to the newspapers, became centers of propaganda, not for salvation in heaven but for the rights of man on earth. Ezra Stiles, a gentle Puritan clergyman from Newport, showed a seer's gift of prophecy when he summed up colonial reaction.

"The Stamp Act," wrote the future President of Yale University, "has diffused a disgust through the colonies and laid the basis of an alienation which will never be healed."

The Stamp Act became effective on All Saints' Day, November 1, 1765. Nowhere on the continent of America was a stamp to be found. Every distributor had been forced to resign his post in fear of life and property.

Fourteen boxes of stamps had arrived in Boston Harbor for distribution throughout New England. With no one to receive the consignment, they were gathering mold within the dark walls of Castle William.

When stamps for Pennsylvania, New Jersey and Maryland arrived at Philadelphia, every American ship along the two-mile stretch of docks on the banks of the Delaware River lowered its flag to half-mast. The Quaker city remained quiet, save for the mournful ringing of its many church bells. The captain of the British merchant ship could find no one to unload the hateful cargo. Customs authorities finally transferred the stamps to an armed sloop for safekeeping.

In New York, warnings were hung on every lamp post.

> Pro Patria
> > The first Man that Either distributes or makes use of Stampt Paper let him take care of his House, Person, & Effects.
>
> Vox Populi.
> > We dare!

Here too, the parcels of stamps were put aboard a man o'war for safekeeping.

Without stamps, no legal business could be conducted. Every court in the colonies was closed. No ship could leave port, no newspaper could be printed. In Rhode Island, patriotic young ladies refused to listen to proposals of marriage because of the stamp tax on licenses. Everywhere government and business ground to a halt. The colonies were in a virtual state of anarchy.

Rebellion Postponed

The Sons of Liberty assumed *de facto* governing authority. From New London, on Christmas Day, they announced a formal Union in Arms. Still vowing allegiance to their sovereign lord, George III, they declared themselves prepared to defend their liberties with arms if necessary.

Merchants and shipmasters were first to break the impasse. Every wharf and anchorage along the Atlantic seaboard had filled up with vessels unable to get clearance, and idle sailors and stevedores became potential troublemakers in every port. Late in 1765, John Hancock set the example by ordering his *Boston Packet* to set sail without stamped clearance. The captain carried letters to the merchant's friends in London urging them to exert themselves for repeal of the Stamp Act, "or we are gone people."

By the new year, ports were buzzing with activity. British navy ships watched helplessly. What use to seize a vessel when no court south of Halifax remained open to prosecute the owner and captain?

Colonial courts reopened slowly and newspapers resumed publication on unstamped paper, whipping up sentiment for transaction of business without stamps and for tightening the boycott of British goods.

"Had it not been for the continual informations of the Press," wrote one commentator, "a junction of all the people . . . would have been scarcely conceivable."

Britain's desperate economic plight, which the Stamp Act had been calculated to alleviate, had been worsened by the American boycott. Petitions flowed into Parliament from merchants in English ports predicting "utter ruin" of their commerce unless they were given "such relief as to the House shall seem expedient."

Rockingham's ministry sought a way to repeal the Stamp Act without seeming to back down. Yet when King George addressed the opening session of the House of Commons on January 14, 1766, he referred only vaguely to "matters of importance in America." Doubtless the monarch was distracted by the recent death of his younger brother.

In the vaulted chamber, the members lounged listlessly. Many still wore their greatcoats, boots and spurs, evidently hoping to return soon to their own firesides. Yet they waited, munching apples and cracking nuts, for the greatest of all commoners, William Pitt, had written a member earlier in the month. "If I can crawl or be carried, I will deliver my mind and heart upon the state of America."

True to his word, William Pitt was carried into the House chamber on a litter. His eyes glittered with feverish anger as he listened to his brother-in-law, George Grenville, defend his stamp tax.

"Great Britain protects America," declared Grenville. "America is bound to yield obedience! When were Americans emancipated?"

Pitt raised an emaciated hand in a signal that he wished to speak. Lifted to his feet, he bowed painfully to the Speaker. His robes hung loose on his wasted body, but the familiar rich voice carried to the last row of benches.

"Americans are the sons, not the bastards of England!" he cried. "Taxation is no part of the governing or legislative power. Taxes are a voluntary gift and grant of the Commons." The imperious, hawklike gaze swept the company. "By whom is America represented here?

"I have been charged with giving birth to sedition in America. I rejoice that America has resisted. . . . The gentleman asks, when were the colonies emancipated. But I desire to know"— Pitt's voice was a roar now; his beaklike nose quivered with rage—"when were they made slaves?

"I beg leave to tell the House what is really my opinion." The great man paused. His trembling hands grasped the bench before him, but his voice was firm. "It is that the Stamp Act be repealed absolutely, totally and immediately."

The battle over repeal raged for two months in the House of Commons. My Lord Rockingham's private secretary—a 37-year-old Irishman named Edmund Burke, for whom the Prime Minister had wangled a pocket-borough seat—delivered an impassioned plea for repeal. Like most of his countrymen, he linked the liberties of Ireland with those of America and wished "success to the Sons of Liberty."

In this maiden speech before Commons, Edmund Burke showed a remarkable gift of oratory. Even learned Samuel Johnson, who considered Americans "a race of convicts" was forced to admit that the performance of the unknown Irishman "filled the town with wonder." Unfortunately no one bothered to take notes.

On January 28, the ministry played its trump card. Dr. Benjamin Franklin was brought before a Committee of the Whole House to supply additional testimony respecting New World developments.

Somber in rusty homespun, Franklin spoke of the "altered mood" in the colonies since 1763. He emphasized that the distinction between external and internal taxes had always been fundamental to the colonists. Now, he told the members, he heard many arguments that there is no difference—"that if you have no right to tax them internally, you have none to tax them externally, or to make any other law to bind them. At present, they do not reason, so, but in time they may...."

So eager were the Whigs to quell the growing anti-American sentiment in the House that they made the aging, bespectacled sage of Philadelphia appear like a "Master examined before a parcel of schoolboys."

Nor would the military force suggested by some help acceptance of the tax, Dr. Franklin concluded.

"They cannot force a man to take stamps who chuses to do without them. They will not find a rebellion," he cautioned, "but they may indeed make one."

By March 18, the Repeal Bill had passed both houses of Parliament. The news, when it reached them, set off a round of celebrations throughout the colonies.

In Boston, citizens marched with the Sons of Liberty to deck the Liberty Tree with lanterns. On top of the huge elm was propped an enormous cut-out of George III, "resembling a Dutch widow in a short frock."

From his brightly lighted mansion on Beach Hill, John Hancock looked down upon the festivities on Boston Common. He sent his servants with pipes of Madeira for the rejoicing townsfolk. Meanwhile, the "genteel part of town" pushed into his parlor, and that of James Otis nearby, to drink a toast to repeal.

Plans were made to erect statues of William Pitt on New York's Battery as well as in front of Boston's Town House.

The joyous revels drowned out the high-flown phrases of the Declaratory Act which accompanied repeal, and reaffirmed Parliament's right to "make laws and statutes of sufficient force and validity to bind the colonies and people of America . . . in all cases whatsoever."

A few thoughtful men, like George Mason of Virginia, realized the implications of the Declaratory Act. As far as Parliament was concerned, Americans had no rights at all. But Governor Francis Bernard of Massachusetts echoed the fear of many loyal British colonists when he declared that repeal had made "the authority of Great Britain in America contemptible thereafter."

Certainly the colonists were united as never before.

Rebellion Postponed

Exulted John Adams: "That enormous engine, fabricated by the brutish Parliament, for battering down all the Rights and Liberties of America, I mean the Stamp Act, has raised and spread, through the whole Continent, a Spirit that will be recorded to our Honour, with all future Generations."

In 1766, that spirit was burgeoning in the various colonial assemblies.

Repeal of the Stamp Act had reduced Britain's revenue from America to a pittance while administrative and military costs soared to £400,000 per year. Colonial assemblies levied the taxes to pay civil officials. But the people of Britain had to pay to arm, clothe, feed and transport British troops for the defense of the colonies.

When, in 1764, the American Commander-in-Chief, General Sir Thomas Gage, had requested that England's ancient Billeting or Mutiny Act be extended to the colonies, only a few Quakers like John Dickinson had objected. The cost of protection was small. Communities in which troops were stationed were asked to provide for their quartering and to furnish the soldiers with certain necessities such as soap, candles, firewood, cooking utensils, salt, vinegar and small beer or cider.

The demands were greatest in New York, strategic center of Britain's colonies and headquarters of the overseas army. In December, 1765, General Gage expected fresh troops for the relief of frontier garrisons. During the changeover he would need additional barracks and provisions.

The New York Assembly refused the General's request. The assemblymen made it clear that they did not wish to deprive the King's Own of necessities. They wanted the provisions they granted to be considered a gift from the colony rather than meek compliance with a demand of Parliament. The matter was put to the vote, and limited provisions were provided for but with the understanding that the colony be repaid. At the same time, New York merchants sent a petition to the government in London asking that all the navigation and trade laws be scrapped so they might trade freely with the whole world.

Across the Hudson River in Jersey, Governor William Franklin, was plagued with similar problems. He attempted to explain the colonial point of view to the Secretary of State in London:

"... They look upon the Act of Parliament for quartering soldiers in America, to be virtually as much an act for laying taxes on the inhabitants as the Stamp Act, and more partial, as troops [are] kept in a few of the colonies, where by the others [are] exempted from the expense."

Out along the Proclamation Line there was unrest too. The "considerable military force" sent to protect the settlers, as well as the Indian hunting grounds, was causing deep resentment amongst frontiersmen. British troops were under orders to prevent white settlers from penetrating westward before formal disposition of the lands could be made. But the endless forests and mountain fastnesses were like a giant sieve.

"The line will never hold," declared Virginia's Royal Governor, "because Americans would move on, even from Paradise."

Investors in both England and America agreed. George Washington, head of the Virginia Company, which claimed the whole Ohio Valley by original charter rights, considered the Proclamation Line "a temporary expedient to quiet the minds of the Indians. Any person who neglects the present opportunity of hunting out good lands and marking them will never regain it.

Western problems were of no concern in Boston. Parliament had demanded that Massachusetts Bay make compensation to the victims of the Stamp Act riots. For once, conservatives from the countryside agreed with the Boston liberty men that certain conditions be met before any losses were repaid. The chief demand was a general amnesty for all convicted of taking part in the riots.

The Massachusett's legislature admired and condoned New York's stand in the matter of the Quartering Act. By a united show of resourcefulness, the colonies had negated Parliament's stamp tax. Now, by refusing to comply with Parliament's demands before first putting the matter to a vote, they indicated that they thought of colonial assemblies as independent legislatures within the Empire.

VI

THE GOOD SHIP LIBERTY

> *"He has dissolved Representative Houses..."*

WHILE colonial assemblies flexed their legislative muscles, the government in London was playing a game of musical chairs. A statesmanlike ministry might have worked out a constitutional arrangement with the colonies. The idea of a colonial federation under the Crown was popular on both sides of the Atlantic.

Lord Rockingham's ministry fell apart of its own weakness that summer of 1766. King George, with a flash of rare wisdom, called William Pitt out of retirement to form a new government. Swallowing his own dislike of the "Great Commoner," George even gave him a title. As Earl of Chatham, Pitt formed a mosaic ministry, a combination of "all the talents" calculated to please all parties.

Before the old soldier could implement any of his schemes to strengthen the British Empire, he was forced once more by the pain of his gout to retire to Bath. Into the spotlight of the new government was thrust a flamboyant figure—Chancellor of the Exchequer Charles Townshend, better known to his friends about town as "Champagne Charlie."

Townshend was a large, boisterous man whose most brilliant speeches were made under the influence of the sparkling beverage from which came his nickname. Ambitious and vain, he was sometimes called the "Weathercock" too, for he was as mercurial in politics as he was charming socially. He had, for instance, vigorously supported Grenville's stamp tax. A year later, he voted for repeal. Now chance had placed real power within his grasp.

When the British Parliament reconvened in November, 1766, there were "nothing but riots and insurrections over the whole country, on account of the high price of provisions—in particular, corn."

Signs of depression were everywhere in England. Merchants groaned under excessive duties, artisans complained of unfair foreign competition. The landed gentry, with greatest representation in the Commons, were demanding a reduction of their land tax. George Grenville, still a formidable leader in the House, pushed through the tax reduction, thereby slicing half a million pounds from Townshend's prepared budget. Somehow the deficit had to be made up or Townshend knew his ministry was doomed.

"I know a mode by which a revenue may be drawn from America without offense," the weathercock Chancellor blithely declared.

Townshend used Benjamin Franklin's own distinction between external and internal taxes to work out his scheme. Duties would be levied on a number of items that colonials customarily imported from England. These so-called luxuries included five varieties of glass, white and red lead and painters' colors, silks, tea and sixty-seven grades of paper. Carefully omitted from the list were such essentials as salt, coal, hemp and fishhooks.

The levies on each item were small. The revenue expected from the duties was a trivial £40,000, less than a tenth of the income lost by the reduction of the land tax. The amount was a drop in the bucket compared with the cost of government in the American colonies alone.

But other provisions of Townshend's Revenue Bill insured that these duties, unlike earlier ones, would be collected. A resident Board of Customs Commissioners was created, independently responsible for the collection of duties and the enforcement of American port laws. New vice-admiralty courts at Boston, Philadelphia and New York were authorized to try those accused under the new trade laws *without benefit of jury.*

General search warrants, the writs of assistance so abhorred in England as well as in her colonies, were revived to aid customs enforcement.

Most alarming to colonial leaders was the provision of the Townshend Act that the new revenues be used to pay the salaries of governors, judges and other royal officials in the colonies. To expect colonial assemblies to comply with such an edict was like asking them to assist at their own death rites. Only by keeping a firm grip on the purse strings had the assemblies been able to control the servants of the Crown sent to govern them.

A companion act suspended the New York Assembly until such time as it should comply with the letter of the Mutiny Act.

Parliament voted the Townshend Act into law on July 2, 1767, and approved the suspension of New York's Assembly three days later.

In September, before the revenue plan went into effect, London's *bon vivant,* Charles Townshend, dropped dead of diphtheria. He went to his grave believing himself to be a brilliant lawmaker.

Once again, like guests at an Alice-in-Wonderland tea party, His Majesty's ministers shifted places. The Duke of Grafton, an earnest young man of mediocre talents, moved into Townshend's office as Chancellor of the Exchequer. Grafton inherited as well the role of acting Prime Minister.

Lord Chatham, the giant who might have held the colonies for Britain, had suffered a complete breakdown. He sat speechless in his darkened room at Bath while little men fumbled with the problems of the Empire.

Colonial printers were first to react to the Townshend Act. The colonies produced little paper, and the levies on sixty-seven grades of the imported article would send printing costs soaring. Yet the Townshend duties, as "external" taxes, were constitutionally legal. Newsmen directed their attack at the arbitrary suspension of the New York legislature. The *Boston Gazette* called Parliament's action a "shocking" encroachment on colonial rights.

"If our legislative authority can be suspended whenever we refuse obedience to laws we never consented to," theorized an anonymous writer for that paper, "we may as well acknowledge ourselves slaves."

On the whole, however, Governor Bernard noted "a general Abhorrence of the inflammatory Papers expressed thro' the Town."

Even James Otis was calm though disapproving.

"The tax," warned the lawyer in an open letter to the *Gazette*, "is undoubtedly at present the matter of grievance, and this I think a great one. But redress is to be fought in a legal and constitutional way."

Before the Act was to go into effect on November 20, Sam Adams called a town meeting. A paper was drawn up urging the people of Massachusetts to do without "foreign superfluities." The meeting voted to ask citizens throughout Massachusetts Bay to pledge themselves not to purchase any of a long list of luxury items. At the same time the people were asked to take "all prudent and legal measures to encourage the produce and manufactures of the province."

"Save your Money, and save your Country!" exhorted the press throughout the northern colonies. *The Newport Mercury*, like *The Boston Gazette*, offered free advertising to local weavers.

Governor Bernard began to sense that he was sitting on a powder keg, needing only a spark to blow it sky high, Throughout the summer and autumn, Bernard's reports to London became increasingly hysterical. He declared his very life was in danger.

The native-born Lieutenant-Governor, Thomas Hutchinson, was more reasonable but no less alarming in his estimate of the situation. He decried the "levelling" behavior of the Bostonians. Thomas Hutchinson loyally declared the back-country residents to be conservative and quiet, but in his opinion the radical Whigs of the port city were out for nothing less than independence.

So the eyes of official London were on Boston as the ripple of nonimportation agreements spread to other colonial ports. Meanwhile, real opposition to the Townshend Act was mobilized from an unexpected quarter, the peaceful Quaker city of Philadelphia.

Between December 2, 1767, less than two weeks after the duties went into effect, and February 15, 1768, the *Pennsylvania Chronicle* published twelve "Letters from a Farmer in Pennsylvania to the Inhabitants of the British Colonies."

The "Letters" were an eloquent attack on the constitutionality of the Townshend duties based on the philosophy of John Locke. Newspapers throughout the colonies reprinted the essays. Put into pamphlet form, the Letters sold like a popular novel.

No one believed that a farmer had written the learned essays. The identity of the author remained a point of argument for some time before it became generally known that it was John Dickinson, the same London-schooled barrister who had denounced the Quartering Act.

Dickinson displayed a reverential respect for British liberty. His letters dignified opposition to "twopenny" duties by raising the debate to a discussion of the rights of men—

The Good Ship Liberty • 71

especially Englishmen. The cause of liberty, he declared, is "a case of too much dignity to be sullied by turbulence and tumult."

But, warned the "farmer," "We *cannot be* HAPPY, *without being* FREE. . . . We cannot be free, *without being secure in our property*. . . . *We* cannot be secure in our property, *if, without our consent, others may, as by right, take it away.*

"Anger produces anger," he warned. "We have an excellent prince . . . a generous, sensible and humane nation, to whom we may apply. . . . If, however, our applications to His Majesty and the Parliament prove ineffectual, let us then take another step, by withholding all the advantages Great Britain has been used to receive from us. . . . Let us all be united with one spirit in one cause!"

It was that last phrase that alerted royal officials to danger.

"He has articulated a Bill of Rights in the Opinion of the Americans," Governor Bernard warned the ministry. "Parliament may enact Declaratory Acts as many as they please; but they must not expect any real obedience."

The *Farmer's Letters* prompted every colonial assembly to issue an official resolution condemning the Townshend Act. Petitions poured into Whitehall, from the colonies as well as from British merchants, who again saw their trade threatened. The movement to boycott imports swept the Atlantic seaboard. Homespun fabrics returned to fashion, and lamb once again disappeared from colonial dinner tables. Now the Yale students added all foreign liquors to their previous ban on Madeira wines, while Harvard men swore off tea.

James Otis had received an advance text of the *Farmer's Letters* from John Dickinson with an accompanying note.

"Whenever the Cause of American Freedom is to be

vindicated," urged the Quaker lawyer, "I look towards the Province of Massachusetts Bay. She must, as she has hitherto done, first kindle the Sacred Flame. . . ."

The Boston Patriots did not disappoint Dickinson. Samuel Adams drafted a Circular Letter to send to London and all the colonial assemblies. Referring to the dissolution of the New York legislature, because of its refusal to comply with the terms of the Mutiny Act, he pointed out: "Such a restriction throughout the colonies would be a short and easy method of annihilating the legislative powers in America."

Perhaps it was the idea of united action among the colonies that upset the new Secretary of State, Lord Hillsborough. Perhaps it was the letter from the customs commissioners, newly landed in Boston, that arrived by the same boat.

"Unless the hand of government is strengthened," the customs officers complained, "we are powerless to carry out our duties."

Hillsborough scurried off to the palace to show the letters to King George. The other ministers might wish to walk easy with the colonials, but not "Wills Hills." He was only too happy to express His Majesty's displeasure with a Circular Letter of his own.

Governor Bernard was ordered to dissolve the Massachusetts General Court if its offensive resolution was not publicly rescinded. Other colonial assemblies must "take no notice" of the Massachusetts letter, "which will be treating it with the contempt it deserves," Hillsborough concluded. He also alerted General Gage in New York that troops might be necessary to keep peace in Boston.

Once again, it was John Hancock who led active resistance to the new duties. From the beginning he vowed that the new customs officers would not be allowed "to go even on board any of my London ships." His resolve was soon tested.

On April 7, 1768, Hancock's sloop *Lydia*, out of London, dropped anchor in Boston Harbor a few meters off Long Wharf. Two tidewaiters immediately boarded her to search for tea, paper or other dutiable goods. The angry owner, alerted by dockworkers, was aboard almost as soon as the tidewaiters. He ordered Captain James Scott not to allow the watchers below decks. The customs men departed as a threatening crowd gathered on the wharf.

A month later, on May 9, Hancock's sloop *Liberty* put in to Boston. Rumor was that she carried 100 pipes of Madeira wine. A tidesman boarded her before she was made fast to Long Wharf. Hancock's stevedores were already preparing to swarm aboard, eager to unload the *Liberty* before sundown.

"You can't unload until you've cleared customs," the tidewaiter informed the captain.

The captain whistled up two crewmen and ordered them to usher the customs official below decks. There they locked the man in a closet. For three hours, according to his later testimony, he heard tramping and bumping and the squeal of cranes. When he was released, the ship was empty.

John Hancock declared and paid duty on twenty-five casks of wine, a mere fraction of the suspected cargo. Once again the customs officers bided their time.

Early in June, HMS *Romney*, a warship of fifty guns out of Halifax, sailed in to Boston Harbor and anchored a cable's length from shore. Immediately, the customs officers descended on the *Liberty*, now loaded with whale oil and tar, bound for England. Vessel and cargo were seized. Armed marines in a longboat towed the *Liberty* under the guns of the *Romney*, while Hancock was arrested and charged with smuggling.

The customs officers chose the worst time of day for their seizure, when dockworkers were just starting home. Word spread through the whole dingy waterfront area. Soon the crowd on Long Wharf had grown to a menacing mob. The men waited outside the Customs Offices until the Collector, Joseph Harrison, and the Comptroller, Benjamin Hallowell, emerged.

"They were followed to their houses, and their windows broke," reported Lieutenant-Governor Hutchinson. A "pleasure" boat belonging to Harrison was dragged to the Common and burned.

The next day the customs commissioners retired by barge to the *Romney*.

On that same June day in 1768, Governor Bernard told the Massachusetts General Court that it must rescind the Circular Letter or be dissolved. On June 30, after a weeklong debate, the legislators voted not to back down.

The following day, July 1, 1768, Governor Bernard dissolved the House of Representatives of the Crown Colony of Massachusetts Bay by order of His Majesty George III—but not before a committee had been appointed to frame an additional petition to King George "praying that His Majesty would be graciously pleased to remove His Excellency, Francis Bernard, Esq., from the government of this province."

VII

NONE BUT A SLAVE

". . . For depriving us . . . of Trial by Jury . . ."

GOVERNOR Bernard's alarming reports of conditions in the port of Boston, coupled with those of his Lieutenant-Governor and the customs commissioners, had caused a quick reaction in London. Lord Hillsborough, the excitable Secretary of State for the colonies, promptly dispatched two regiments of regulars from Ireland and two from Halifax to put down the insurrection, which, he believed, threatened to engulf the whole Bay Colony.

All over London in the summer of 1768 there was talk of treason in America. Prophets of doom insisted that the arrival of troops would arouse the colonists to full-scale rebellion. Stocks on the London exchange tumbled.

The certain approach of the troops had indeed alarmed the patriots of Boston. There was talk of resisting the landing. The ancient tall pole on Beacon Hill, used to signal the countryside of approaching danger, was equipped once more with a turpentine barrel ready to be fired. Sam Adams persuaded the Boston selectmen to call a provincial convention, hoping for a show of resistance.

But when the British men-of-war and the transports were sighted off Nantasket on September 28, the town was quiet. The men of Massachusetts Bay felt powerless in the face of cannon.

About noon on Saturday, October 1, 1768, British regulars began landing on Long Wharf. Paul Revere watched from his shop door as they "formed and marched with insolent parade, drums beating, fifes playing, up King Street."

Silent people lined the way as a thousand soldiers in scarlet coats, with sabers flashing in the bright autumn sunlight, strutted along Queen Street to Tremont and wheeled onto the Common. Deployed across the rolling green pastureland, the companies of foot soldiers in scarlet and white, the platoons of Grenadiers with towering hats and the light artillery were a brave and awesome sight.

The drums and fifes were silent. The townsfolk stared at the soldiers, and the soldiers stared impassively back. They saw a small provincial English town and a band of curious citizens—citizens whom they had been sent to "pacify."

Colonials, like their English forebears, disliked and distrusted a standing army. The officers were often arrogant fops whose commissions and promotions were bought rather than earned. Most despised their work and the men they were meant to lead. Indeed those men were, for the most part, brutes, driven to the Army by extreme poverty or fear of prison or the noose. They would as cheerfully cut their superiors' throats as those of the enemy, but for fear of the lash.

Yet the redcoats had one talent much in demand across the colony. They knew the Manual of Arms and the art of war. Within the first week, forty soldiers disappeared into the beckoning countryside, doubtless tempted by the offer of a post as drillmaster in some remote village of western Massachusetts.

Most of the deserters were caught and returned to stand savage punishment. In final desperation, Colonel William Dalrymple ordered the execution of one fugitive. From that day, his command that soldiers must not fraternize with civilians was strictly obeyed. The redcoats walked in pairs, heads held high. They jostled Bostonians off the sidewalks.

The clomp of heavy boots on the cobblestone streets, the bright coats everywhere, the shrill notes of the fife and rattle of drums from dawn until dusk rasped the public nerves.

"A regiment was exercised by Major Small on Brattle Square directly in front of my house," wrote John Adams that winter. "Their appearance in Boston was a strong proof to me that the determination in Great Britain to subjugate us was too deep and inveterate ever to be altered by us. For everything we could do was misrepresented, and nothing we could say was credited."

The soldiers had nothing to do that winter but march and countermarch, to clatter through the streets at night on patrol, disturbing peaceful citizens, challenging those who ventured abroad. This daily and nightly occurrence infuriated Sam Adams.

". . . to be called to account by a common soldier," he complained in an open letter to the *Gazette*, "or any soldier, is a badge of slavery which none but a slave will bear."

He was sure the town would be placed under martial law. Strangely it was not. The regiments remained a police force subject to the jurisdiction of the civil courts.

Early in November, 1768, the customs commissioners who had fled to Castle William after the Liberty riots moved back to town with their families and staffs. Their return reopened the case of John Hancock's sloop, *Liberty*. Hancock engaged John Adams as counsel, a measure of the young lawyer's growing reputation.

"There were few days through the whole winter when I was not summoned to attend the Court of Admiralty," John Adams recorded. "It seemed as if officers of the Crown were determined to examine the whole town as witnesses."

Not a single witness would testify against John Hancock at his trial for smuggling. There was not a shred of evidence, his lawyer pointed out, that Hancock was even aware of the "frolic"—the smuggling of casks of wine ashore in the night. In the absence of any provable facts, John Adams based his defense on the rights of Englishmen under Magna Carta, especially the right to trial by jury.

"Is there a brand of infamy, of degradation and disgrace fixed upon every American?" Adams asked the court. To try a man without benefit of jury, as in the Admiralty Courts, he went on, "is it not a repeal of Magna Carta as far as America is concerned?"

The trial dragged on through the winter, "a painful drudgery" to lawyer Adams. In march, 1769, the Crown dismissed the case for want of evidence.

While Boston chafed under occupation, the government in London pondered the "treasonable and desperate" state of the colony of Massachusetts Bay. Governor Bernard was urged to secure the fullest information concerning "all treasons and misprision of treason." In February, 1769, it was decided that the "wicked and designing men" who were stirring up the colonists against king and Parliament should be brought to England for trial under an ancient treason statute of Henry VIII. That headstrong monarch had devised an airtight law to rid himself of opposition.

Heading the king's list of "wicked and designing men" were the Boston patriots James Otis, Jr., Samuel Adams and Thomas Cushing.

The middle and southern colonies had not reacted violently to the Townshend duties. Philadelphia merchants were almost a year behind their fellows of Boston in clamping down on British imports. Even then, the Sons of Liberty needed to keep backsliders in line.

In Virginia and the Carolinas, the duties had little effect on the tobacco and rice economy. But the proposed law to transport Americans to England for trial was calcu-

None But A Slave

lated to prod all the colonists to rebellion. The horrid image of American heads elevated on a pike over Tyburn Gate in London was too dreadful for even the most conservative to entertain. In Virginia, opposition to the home government found new leadership among wealthy tidewater planters such as George Washington and George Mason.

Washington had always concerned himself primarily with county affairs. He did not even attend the stormy assembly session when Virginia first joined the other colonies in protesting the Townshend duties. Now he and George Mason, his neighbor at Gunston Hall, drew up a nonimportation plan for Virginia.

"At a time when our lordly masters in Great Britain will be satisfied with nothing less than the depreciation of American freedom," wrote the squire of Mount Vernon, "it seems highly necessary that something should be done to avert the stroke and maintain the liberty which we have derived from our ancestors. . . .

"No man should scruple or hesitate a moment to use arms in defense of so valuable a blessing . . . yet arms, I would beg leave to add, should be the last . . . the dernier resort. . . ."

The tall patrician burgess and soldier was armed only with a sheaf of documents on the morning of May 17, 1769, as he waited on the square before the Capitol at Williamsburg for the new Governor, Lord Botetourt. The king's representative in his gilded coach was not the object of farmer Washington's interest so much as the team of cream-colored horses that were the pride of Williamsburg.

"Some day I shall have such a team," thought Washington as he took his seat.

In the small chamber where Patrick Henry had first thrown down the gauntlet of rebellion, there was an electric feeling of expectation that May morning. Washington noted that the eloquent firebrand seemed silent and withdrawn. As always, suave, meticulous Peyton Randolph dominated the assembly. One of Virginia's most conservative statesmen, he held the confidence of his associates whether they agreed with his views or not.

George Washington's gaze rested appreciatively on the slight, erect figure of George Wythe. The learned lawyer was a staunch defender of colonial rights within the framework of the British Empire. He was talking excitedly with a lean, youthful redhead, whom Washington did not recognize. The new burgess appeared to be inches taller than Washington himself, certainly over six feet.

"Who is the athletic-looking fellow with the courtly manner?" Washington inquired of his neighbor.

"That's Tom Jefferson of Monticello," was the reply. "He's a student of Wythe's and almost as learned. That young man bears watching."

The squire of Mount Vernon bowed warmly to his old friends the Lees, Francis Lightfoot and Richard Henry. The last had been educated at the Inns of Court in London. His golden tongue had earned him the title "Cicero of the House." He was an aristocratic and wealthy planter, and his revolutionary ideas shocked other members of his class. Richard Henry Lee was an ardent admirer of Sam Adams and his coterie of Boston patriots. His quiet, forceful speeches had drawn young burgesses to his standard. With a wave of his crippled left hand, Lee rejected humble petitions to Parliament and the king. Colonial rights would never be won that way, he counseled.

The burgesses were unanimous this morning in approving "an humble, dutiful and loyal address" to George III, "praying the royal interposition in favor of the violated rights of America."

Governor Botetourt was prepared for the action. He

immediately summoned the legislators to his Council Chamber, and there read an angry order dissolving the Assembly. Without a word, the representatives of the people of Virginia dispersed to their rooms and boarding houses.

That evening, twenty-eight burgesses met in the Apollo Room of the Raleigh Tavern, where Patrick Henry had drawn up the first Virginia Resolves. In this room, most of the men were accustomed to relax, to dine and dance and flirt with the ladies. Now they met as partners in a conspiracy to resist an order of the British Parliament. George Washington presented the nonimportation agreement that he and Mason had drawn up, and it was accepted almost as written.

Nonimportation associations were formed in every county of Virginia, beginning with the wealthy tidewater regions. Committees were organized to supervise and rigidly enforce the nonimportation pledge. In South Carolina, Christopher Gadsden sparked similar agreements with his series of "Letters of a Freeman" in the *South Carolina Gazette*.

Gadsden himself set an example by attending his wife's funeral in a homespun suit. A soft cap replaced his wig.

The enforcement committees were rigid and uncompromising, yet there was surprisingly little violence or injustice. The ban on British imports was so orderly and widespread that any laughter in London over the boycott laid down by those comic rustics of America was silenced. Throughout the South, the beloved silks and wigs, ornate coaches and imported mounts became taboo. English manufacturers and merchants were the poorer by £900,000 worth of trade.

Hand in hand went a campaign to encourage the manufacture of home products. George Washington had long advocated more diversity of crops for Virginia, where the widespread cultivation of tobacco kept the colony economically chained to English markets. He grew corn and wheat and a number of other products at Mount Vernon. His weavers and blacksmiths now set the tune as, up and down the colonies, spinning wheels and looms whirred and sang, anvils and foundries pounded—a symphony of independence from British goods.

In Europe, the courage and steadfastness of the colonials aroused respect. The American was depicted in simple homespun, avoiding British products, living in windowless, unpainted houses. Every Frenchman of letters prided himself on being a "frankliniste."

The object of their adulation, Benjamin Franklin, wrote to his son William, Governor of New Jersey: "All Europe appears to be on our side of the question. . . . I find myself confirmed in opinion that no middle doctrine can be well maintained. . . . The Parliament has the right to make all laws for us, or it has the power to make no laws for us. . . ."

British government officials were thinking along the same lines. Perhaps some friend of America recalled Franklin's earlier warning that, in attempting to force the colonists to accept Parliament's decrees, they might indeed make a rebellion where none had been before.

The impact of America's growing resistance fell on a ministry without a head, floundering without direction. Early in 1770, William Pitt was replaced as Lord Privy Seal by the popular and esteemed Chancellor of the Exchequer, Lord North.

Frederick, Earl of Guilford and eighth Lord North, was a rotund and pop-eyed man, renowned for his good sense and quiet humor. He was a hard worker, a man most likely to give the British Empire the sort of leadership it so sorely needed. Certainly North would not sit by passively and watch the dismemberment of the empire.

Lord North assumed office in March, 1770. His first act was to ask Parliament to repeal the Townshend duties. He wished to take from the colonies any legitimate ground for claiming to be oppressed.

At the same time, he reaffirmed the principle of the Declaratory Act by retaining the tax on tea— "as a mark of the supremacy of Parliament, and an efficient declaration of their right to govern the colonies."

North's repeal bill was reported to Parliament on March 5, 1770.

VIII

THE GATHERING STORM

"He has kept among us in times of peace, Standing Armies..."

MONDAY, March 5, 1770, was a bitter cold day in Boston. Soft new snow lay deep on the cobbled streets, muffling the heavy tread of soldiers' boots as they tramped their constant patrols. Yet the aura of peace that enveloped the silent town hid a festering wound of hate rubbed raw by two years of occupation.

Besides the hordes of redcoats crowding Boston's streets and disfiguring its beloved Common, His Majesty's warships surrounded the port. The custom commission's revenue vessels patrolled the whole Atlantic coastline waiting to pounce on merchant vessels. Worse than their search for contraband were the press gangs off the battleships, who could claim any able-bodied seaman or fisherman as a deserter and "press" him into the Royal Navy.

The press gangs haunted coastal waters and dockside taverns, causing every seafaring man to walk in terror.

While the king's officers were entertained in wealthy colonial homes and newspapers announced their frequent betrothals to colonial belles, common soldiers suffered every sort of indignity at the hands of town toughs. Small boys pelted them with garbage and worse. They were jostled off bridges or pushed headlong into the mud. Every tavern in town was the scene of nightly brawls. "Lobsterback" was the mildest epithet hurled at them.

Forbidden to reply with blows, the redcoats made up

ditties ridiculing the provincials. The favorite time for a songfest was the Sabbath, when most colonials were in services. Then the beleaguered soldiers would gather outside churches and meeting houses to drown out the Puritan hymns with filthy rhymes bellowed off-key. "Yankee Doodle" was exceptional since it had a semblance of a tune and its lyrics were goodnatured.

An added irritation was the invasion of the British regulars into the job market. Despite unemployment due to a sharp decline in trade with Great Britain, the regulars were encouraged to fill in their spare time and fatten their purses by seeking odd jobs. Whenever a British private sought work he could expect a fight, and the soldiers soon discovered that a cordwainer's knife or a butcher's cleaver, a barrel stave and the wolder stick used in the rope walks were as lethal as a bayonet or cutlass.

By March of 1770, smoldering ill-will was ready to burst into flame. In January, redcoats in New York had cut down the Liberty Pole on the Battery and cut it up for firewood. The enraged Sons of Liberty attacked the soldiers, and in the battle a civilian was impaled on a bayonet and killed. General Gage left Massachusetts to try to solve the crisis in New York. While he was away, violence flared in Boston.

A series of angry incidents was topped off with a pitched battle at Gray's ropewalk on Friday, March 2, started when three off-duty soldiers wandered in seeking work. The rope workers with their heavy wolder sticks were trouncing the soldiers when the owner called on passing officers and civilians to break up the fight.

Cold and snow kept soldier and civilian alike close to the fireside over the weekend. But on Monday night, town toughs and apprentice boys roamed the streets again, while companies of soldiers were out avowedly seeking revenge for Friday's uneven battle. Several citizens were cornered in dark alleys and brutally beaten. Wherever a crowd of "townies" encountered soldiers, a fight broke out.

"Bloody Lobsterbacks! Kill the British boogers!" was the cry. The late-rising moon shone down on several angry groups. Some haunted the barracks on Brattle Street, while others lingered near Faneuil Hall. On the south side of Market Square a lone sentry stood watch in front of the Custom House.

Hugh Montgomery was a mild young peasant boy who had gone into the army because work could not be found at home. He had looked forward to coming to America, where, he had been told, there was opportunity and land for all. He soon concluded that the people of Boston, at least, were wild as the Indians. On this night he withstood the usual pelting of snowballs, oyster shells, coals and sarcasm as long as he could. But when the small group of young boys that was taunting him was joined by a larger crowd of grown men, Montgomery became frightened.

"Town-born, turn-out!" the mob chanted.

Somewhere a church bell began to ring, an alarm calling out all citizens to fight fire.

At the front of the seething crowd was an awesome giant nonchalantly leaning on a stick. To the English country boy, he seemed, with his shining white teeth, like some dark genie. Private Montgomery nervously tried to prime his firelock as he retreated up the Custom House steps. His fingers were numb with cold.

"If he fires he'll die for it!" someone cried.

"I don't care," replied the now terrified redcoat. "If anyone touches me, I'll fire!"

Amid showers of ice and stones, Montgomery leveled his musket at his assailants and bellowed for the main guard.

A block away, Captain Thomas Preston was alert for trouble. He sent a sergeant and six men, who joined Montgomery within seconds. Amid shouts and dares, the sergeant ordered his men to prime and load. Captain Preston arrived to find the soldiers backed up against the wall with loaded muskets leveled at the group of citizens.

Paul Revere, making his way home from the Salutation Tavern, came upon the scene. At the back of the crowd, he heard cool voices entreating those near them to go home. But towards the front could be heard taunting shouts of "Present!" and "Fire!"

"I dare you to fire!"

The six-foot mulatto, Crispus Attucks, who had so frightened young Montgomery, could be seen towering above the mob. Suddenly he raised his stick in what appeared to be a threatening gesture. The soldier in front of him stepped back, slipped on the ice and fell. A musket cracked. Then, in ragged succession, six more shots were fired.

The crowd drew back, silent. Beneath the blue musket smoke, five men lay on the crimson-streaked moonlit snow. Three were dead, two mortally wounded. By this time every bell in town was ringing. The square rapidly filled with soldiers and civilians. Only the timely arrival of Lieutenant-Governor Thomas Hutchinson averted a real massacre, for the soldiers were now primed to fire in earnest.

By sunup, the two wounded citizens were dead. Captain Preston, his sergeant and the seven soldiers were in jail charged with manslaughter, and the patriots had an item of propaganda that all the king's men would find hard to legislate away.

The whole countryside was aroused. People from Charlestown, Cambridge, Malden and Newton streamed into Boston the following day to attend a town meeting at Faneuil Hall. Acting Governor Hutchinson tried to appease them by ordering the regiments to be removed to Castle

William. But the citizens wanted blood, an appetite whetted by the gruesome etching Revere was persuaded to make of the event. Though he protested that the scene he witnessed could hardly be termed a "bloody massacre," this was the title given his work when it appeared in the *Gazette*.

Sam Adams' account spoke movingly of "Innocent Blood Crying to God from the streets of Boston." His cousin John was skeptical. His cool legal mind supposed that the soldiers might, indeed, have acted in self-defense or been confused by the crowd's taunts to fire.

"As God Almighty is my judge, I believe him an innocent man," declared the Irish businessman James Forrest when he asked John Adams to defend Captain Preston.

John Adams knew that his popularity, perhaps even his safety, would be at stake if he undertook the defense of the British soldiers. Yet he believed every man had the right to counsel and a fair trial. Besides, it was imperative to prove to the government in London, eager to bring their own officials home for trial, that any man would be given a fair and honest trial in an American court.

"If Preston thinks he cannot have a fair trial without my assistance," John Adams told Forrest, "then he shall have it."

At the trial, in September, ninety-four witnesses gave testimony against the British soldiers and their captain. John Adams and his cousin, Josiah Quincy, produced witnesses of their own who gave a different version of the events of March 5, 1770. Some insisted that Attucks had actually hit one of the soldiers. All the evidence indicated that Preston and his men had endured extreme provocation, yet it remained impossible to prove that the captain or his sergeant had given an order to fire.

The jury acquitted six of the soldiers outright. Hugh Montgomery and one other, convicted of manslaughter, were allowed to "plead their clergy." Under British criminal law, if a prisoner could read from Scripture, he could be held liable for his crimes. The two prisoners, unable to decipher a word, were branded on their left thumbs and dismissed. The rough, simple men wept openly as they gathered around their colonial advocates to express gratitude for saving them from the noose.

To avoid further outbreaks of violence, a citizens' nightwatch was set. John Adams was a proud member.

"I had the honour to be summoned, in my turn, & attended at the state-house with my musket and bayonet, my broadsword and cartridge box. . . . I know you will laugh at my military figure, but I believe there was not a more obedient soldier in the Regiment. . . ."

By the time of the soldiers' trial in September, 1770, news had reached America that the Townshend duties were repealed, except for that on tea. The act had the effect desired by Lord North. Merchants in colonial ports resumed normal trade with Britain and the colonists turned their attention back to their own internal conflicts.

Both Virginia and Connecticut were squabbling with Pennsylvania over western lands, while New York and New Hampshire carried on a running battle over the boundary between the two colonies.

In North Carolina, strong-minded leaders from the western counties—Scots, Germans and Welshmen, as well as English, joined forces in an attack on the eastern establishment. Calling themselves Regulators, they demanded more representation in the colonial assembly and fewer taxes. The dispute flamed into open warfare in 1771 between the Regulators and troops led by Governor Tryon. The bloody rift between east and west was not to be healed for many years.

Even in Massachusetts, grumbling against royal power was subdued. Samuel Adams, forced out of the Assembly, gathered around him a radical faction that used every opportunity to stir up trouble.

Revenue vessels remained a continuing irritation to merchant ships. Late in 1771, a customs boat towing a prize loaded with undeclared wine and tea up Delaware Bay was boarded by black-faced marauders. The crew of the revenue ship was overpowered, the sails and rigging cut to ribbons. Then the boarding party made off with the seized merchantman and its illegal cargo. Though Governor Penn offered a £200 reward, no clue was forthcoming as to the identity of the attackers.

In June, 1772, another revenue vessel, the *Gaspee*, was burned to the waterline as it lay aground on a sandbar in Narragansett Bay. Obviously the *Gaspee* had been chased aground. Indeed, her commanding officer had been wounded by gunfire. This was wanton destruction of government property and an affront to a king's officer that could not be overlooked. A royal commission was appointed to probe the incident. Again no shred of evidence could be found against the guilty parties, though prominent businessmen of Providence had openly organized the expedition against the revenuer.

That same June of 1772, Governor Hutchinson of Massachusetts, on orders from the home government, announced that hereafter the Crown would pay the Governor's salary, previously paid by the legislature. Later that summer, the Crown provided permanent salaries for Superior Court judges. The action was a warning sign to patriots, who were jealous of every charter right. To make royal officials independent of the domestic legislature clearly exposed "the province to a despotic administration of government."

An emergency town meeting voted into being Sam

The Gathering Storm

Adams' long-nurtured project, the Committee of Correspondence—

> ... to state the rights of the colonists and of this province in particular as men and Christians and as subjects; and to communicate and publish the same to the several towns and to the world as the sense of this town, with the infringements and violations thereof that have been or from time to time may be made.

By November, Boston's twenty-one-member committee had sent letters to all the other Bay Colony towns and to every assembly in America stating their rights and grievances, and exhorting them to create their own Committees of Correspondence. They must not, counseled Boston, "doze or sit supinely indifferent on the brink of destruction."

Virginia patriots felt the same sense of urgency, though for a different reason. They were alarmed by powers of the royal commission appointed to investigate the affairs of the *Gaspee* "to transmit persons accused of offenses committed in AMERICA to places beyond the seas to be tried."

In March, 1773, Thomas Jefferson, Patrick Henry and Richard Henry Lee presented a series of resolutions to the Virginia House of Burgesses urging the appointment of a Committee of Correspondence. They were, explained Jefferson, "sensible that the most urgent of all measures was that of coming to an understanding with all the other colonies."

The Rhode Island House of Deputies had already created its own Committee of Correspondence. In its first letter to sister assemblies the Rhode Island Committee stated "that a firm Union of the Colonies is absolutely necessary for the Preservation of their ancient, legal and constitutional Rights."

The Committees of Correspondence were the foundation of political unity between the colonies—the first and most necessary step to independence. Copies of their correspondence were sent faithfully to the Ministry of Great Britain. Their lordships were apparently too distracted by the impending bankruptcy of the East India Tea Company to heed events in North America.

Every British family of means owned stock in the East India Tea Company. Its failure might cause panic in a country already plagued with depression. During that spring of 1773, Lord North presented to Parliament his Tea Act.

The Tea Act proposed an outright loan to keep the East India Tea Company afloat. All import duties on tea brought to England were to be removed. Company agents would be allowed to export directly to America, thus eliminating English taxes and American middlemen. The Townshend duty on tea in America would offset the Crown's loan to the East India company, yet the duty was so small (threepence per pound) that, with all the other costs removed, East India tea would undercut the smuggled product.

The Tea Act pleased Lord North in every way. The East India Tea Company would become the chief supplier of the beloved weed in America. The duty would enrich crown coffers by £12,000 annually. Best of all, Parliament's right to levy taxes on Americans would be strongly asserted.

In May, 1773, North's Tea Act passed both houses of Parliament with little opposition.

IX

A SALTY BREW

> "... For ... altering fundamentally the Forms of our Governments ..."

TEA was the "idol of America," sipped at least twice daily by a million colonists. Coffee and chocolate might be fancied by some city folk, but they were exotic, expensive drinks. Milk was confined to those lucky few who owned a cow. Not only was tea stimulating and tasty, but it was cheap and easily transported and could be prepared anywhere.

In the forests beyond the mountains, the ubiquitous teapot steamed in every pioneer kitchen and over every trapper's campfire. Even the Indians drank tea, when firewater could not be obtained. A traveler could get a drink of tea just about anywhere in the American settlements.

Much of the tea imbibed by Americans was smuggled through the Dutch Indies. When British customs officers cracked down on the illegal trade, colonials experimented with substitutes rather than pay the duty on tea. Prompted by the Indians, dried raspberry leaves were boiled into a horrid-tasting potion. Others tried a concoction of thyme, sage and sassafras, while the more courageous sampled steeped catnip and pennyroyal.

Sea captains continued to sneak in packets of the forbidden herb for family and friends. The contraband tea was brewed in coffeepots for appearance's sake.

Most colonists might indeed have cheerfully swallowed the tea duty along with their favorite beverage. But the merchants of Newport, New York and Philadelphia who normally handled the London tea trade watched uneasily as the East India Tea Company set up huge warehouses. They were the middlemen whose profit had been eliminated. Only those traders who had loyally opposed the colonial boycott on British goods were chosen now to receive the company's tea.

"What the Parliament could not fleece from us by Taxes, the Crown will by Monopoly!" protested the *Pennsylvania Gazette*.

The fear of a giant monopoly that would totally destroy colonial business was real enough, since the East India Tea Company handled silks, spices, china and calicoes as well as tea.

"The Monopoly on Tea is, I dare say, but a small Part of the Plan they have formed to strip us of our Property," warned John Dickinson.

Resistance to the Tea Act followed much the same pattern as the campaign that had been used against the stamp tax. Through the Committees of Correspondence, Sam Adams ordered a boycott on East India tea. Philadelphia voted to force the company's agents to resign as they had forced the stamp collectors out of office, and other major import centers followed suit.

The press whipped up sentiment by inventing weird and wonderful reasons for avoiding that beverage, which was variously described as the "nauseous draught," "vile growth" and "detestable weed." Some claimed that tea was poisonous, fattening or injurious to teeth, skin and hair.

Dr. Young, a Boston physician, quoted the European opinion that tea drinking was ruinous to health, while patriots insisted that tea was an evil infusion.

"Do not suffer yourself to sip the accursed, dutied STUFF" was the warning spread throughout the colonies,

A Salty Brew

"for if you do, the Devil will immediately enter into you, and you will instantly become a traitor to your country."

Daughters of Liberty, who had once rejected suitors because of the Stamp tax on marriage licenses, now organized non-tea parties. They made a ceremony of emptying their tea cannisters, then gathered around a coffee pot to sign a pledge "not to Conform to that Pernicious Custom of Drinking Tea."

The arrival of the first tea ship set ablaze the smoldering embers of unrest. When the *Dartmouth* arrived in Nantasket Roads, the church bells of Boston tolled out a general muster. Even as the merchantman sailed past the brooding battlements of Castle William into Boston Harbor, on November 27, 1773, the Sons of Liberty were gathering in Faneuil Hall. The meeting voted that the detested tea be returned to London and no duty paid.

A week later the *Eleanor* and the *Beaver* joined the *Dartmouth*. Handbills appeared all over Boston exhorting citizens to resist the landing of any tea. An appeal was sent to Governor Hutchinson asking him to intervene with the customs officials. Hutchinson felt he was being pressured by a "mob" of radicals, and insisted that "the duty must be collected."

The "mob" of radicals was equally intent that American rights be upheld. A guard was placed along the waterfront to prevent the tea from being landed. John Hancock sent riders south to tell the merchants of New York and Philadelphia what Boston was doing. Then, on December 16, the Sons of Liberty held a mass meeting at the Old South Meeting House. Several thousand citizens waited outside in a cold mid-winter drizzle, but soon after noon Sam Adams sent them home.

At dusk, three disciplined groups of men disguised as Mohawk Indians converged on the dock area. Protected by a cordon of citizens stationed along the waterfront, they rowed out to the tea ships in small boats. They were soon lost in the fog that wisped over the darkening harbor. But the creaking of ropes as the "Indians" swarmed aboard the merchantmen was clearly audible in the still moist air. There were war whoops and the crack of hatchets on wood as they breached the tea chests. The gray wavelets lapping along the shore turned muddy ochre and the pungent odor of tea rose in the salty air.

Over three hundred chests of tea were lifted from the ships' holds and dumped into the harbor. Some believed that the ships' sailors helped. Because of the crowds on the quayside no royal official could see who the Indians were, though the disguises barely covered them. Some said they recognized John Hancock by his "ruffles."

News of Boston's "Tea Party" broke the tense calm of seaports to the south. In New York and Philadelphia, the tea ships had been kept far out in the harbor. Now, if only to show solidarity with the men of Boston, New York Sons of Liberty dumped a consignment of tea into the harbor while a band on the quay trumpeted "God Save the King."

To the strains of "Tea Deum," a parody of the traditional victory anthem "Te Deum," or "Thanks Be to God," similar episodes flared along the coast. In New Jersey and Maryland, the tea was burned. Annapolis patriots went so far as to destroy the ship itself, the *Peggy Stewart,* along with its cargo of tea. Only in Charleston (formerly Charles Town) was the tea put ashore, but when patriots dumped some in the river, the city fathers impounded it in a warehouse (where it moldered until long after the revolution).

Many colonists were angered by the destruction of tea shipments, fearing they would be forced to repay the East India Tea Company. Some cargoes were sent back across the Atlantic intact.

The Essex, Massachusetts, *Gazette* even announced the dissolution of that town's Committee of Correspondence by the sober majority of citizens who thought their violent activities might "introduce anarchy, confusion and bloodshed among the people."

John Adams did not agree. Though previously shocked by mob methods of resisting British measures, he had changed his mind.

"This destruction of the tea," he exulted in his diary, "is so bold, so daring . . . , it must have important consequences. . . . It is an epocha in history."

News of the Boston Tea Party took the usual slow route across the Atlantic. Not until the middle of January, 1774, did the reports of the captains of the ships in Boston Harbor reach the government. These, coupled with newspaper accounts quoting the colonial press, and letters from Englishmen and Tories in America, produced a violent swing of public opinion against the colonies.

"*Delenda est Bostoniensis*" echoed the words of Cato. "Boston must be destroyed!"

Lord North was genuinely dumbfounded by the colonists' reaction. He had offered "relief instead of an oppression." Only "New England fanatics" would have rebelled, he insisted.

For two years North had directed Parliament's attention to the East, away from the American colonies, lulling the members and the British public into a false sense that the patriots had changed their position. No one had heeded Ben Franklin's repeated warnings that the ancient Atlantic colonies considered themselves separate states within the Empire, not subject to Britain's Parliament.

The Privy Council determined to humiliate the beloved philosopher and symbol of American patriotism. A public hearing was set for January 29, 1774, that was in effect a trial of both the Massachusetts Bay Colony and its agent.

"All the courtiers were invited as to an entertainment, and there never was such an appearance of privy councillors on any occasion," remembered Franklin.

For over an hour the Solicitor General, Alexander Wedderburn, thundered accusations at the 68-year-old doctor. He had, Wedderburn insisted, plotted the whole project in order to oust Governor Hutchinson and become governor himself. Throughout it all, noted *The London Press*, Dr. Franklin stood "conspicuously erect," a dignified figure in his spotless suit of black Manchester velvet. He wore a "tranquil expression of countenance and he did not suffer the slightest alteration of it to appear."

Wedderburn's accusations seemed to Edmund Burke "beyond all bounds and measure." But the spectacle brought laughter and even applause from the audience as if they were attending a staged event.

On January 31, Benjamin Franklin was dismissed as Postmaster General of the American colonies.

Few paid attention to his statement that he believed his fellow Americans should make reparation for the tea they had destroyed.

Disgraced and out of favor, the elder statesman sadly prepared to return to his native land. During those troubled months early in 1774, he was approached by a rather disreputable-looking young man. Thomas Paine was a sometime pamphleteer who wished to emigrate to America. Franklin decided the writer showed promise and gave him some letters of introduction to newspaper friends in the colonies.

The new disorders in America united North's government in a determination to make no more concessions to the colonies. They agreed that "effectual steps be taken to secure the Dependence of the Colonies on the Mother Country."

A Salty Brew

The dispute, they decided, was no longer about taxation but struck at the very heart of Britain's authority over those "haughty American republicans."

"The King especially had Boston on the brain," recorded one English observer. "To his eyes the capital of Massachusetts was a center of vulgar sedition, bristling with Trees of Liberty, where his enemies went about clothed in homespun, and his friends in tar and feathers."

"We must master them," George declared with rare decisiveness, "or totally leave them to themselves and treat them as aliens."

Any semblance of government by consent gave way to government by coercion when the Boston Port Bill was passed by Parliament in March, 1774. The New England port, whose very existence depended on its trade, was to be closed to all shipping until its citizens paid for the tea destroyed and compensated the revenue officials for the lost duties. Boston was singled out for punishment because, declared one MP, "you will never meet with proper obedience to the laws of this country until you have destroyed that nest of locusts."

Thanks to the Committees of Correspondence, no longer did any American city or colony stand alone. When news of the Port Bill arrived in Boston that May, the sturdy silversmith Paul Revere was immediately dispatched southward, his saddlebags stuffed with copies of the bill. The express rider carried a circular letter from the Boston Committee to all the colonial assemblies, urging them to consider Boston's troubles their own.

"Boston could not support the cause under so severe a trial," added wily Sam Adams in a personal note. "A thought so dishonorable to our brethren can not be entertained, as that this town will now be left to struggle alone."

Even as Revere pounded southward, the frigate *Lively*

sailed into Boston Harbor bringing General Sir Thomas Gage to replace Thomas Hutchinson as Royal Governor of Massachussetts.

General Gage was an amiable, well-intentioned man who had lived, worked and fought in the colonies since 1755. He was married to a colonial girl from New Jersey. Half of Boston turned out despite a spring rain to greet the new governor. Military companies from all over the colony were drawn up in King Street as Colonel John Hancock and his Independent Cadet Corps led the General's party up from Long Wharf.

Blossoming over the waiting crowd like huge May flowers were new contraptions called umbrellas. Made of oiled silk or linen stretched over whalebone ribs, they protected powdered wigs and fine silks from the elements.

The air of gaiety was short-lived. The sympathetic Gage, who might have dealt firmly but fairly with the delicate situation in Boston, found that the London government had made his job impossible.

In Williamsburg, Virginia, news of the Boston Port Bill prompted Thomas Jefferson to suggest to the burgesses that June 1, the day the bill went into effect, should be proclaimed throughout the colonies "a day of fasting, humiliation and prayer."

Governor Dunmore found the proffered resolution so offensive that he dissolved the Assembly. Once again, the more militant members met in "association" at Anthony Hays's popular Raleigh Tavern. The Virginians adopted "an unequivocal stand in the line with Massachusetts."

"The attack on Boston," they declared, "is a most dangerous attempt to destroy the constitutional liberty and rights of all North America."

Meanwhile, Richard Henry Lee penned a personal letter to Samuel Adams.

A Salty Brew

"Do you not think, Sir," wrote Lee, "that the first essential step for our Assembly to take will be an invitation to a general congress as speedily as the nature of the thing will admit?"

A general congress was urged by Committees of Correspondence in Philadelphia, New York and Providence. But to assemble such a body would take time. Meanwhile, gifts of food poured into Boston from the other colonies—rice from Charleston, a thousand barrels of flour from Philadelphia, while New York bravely pledged a ten-year supply of food to the beleaguered port. A flock of more than one hundred sheep was driven overland from Connecticut by the tough old Indian fighter Israel Putnam. Bostonians, instead of being starved into submission, were dining better than ever.

But Lord North was preparing a full-scale reform for the Bay Colony's government. In June, Parliament passed a new package of laws with little opposition. William Pitt, Lord Chatham, made a brilliant plea for leniency in the House of Lords—to no avail.

The Quartering Act was revised and tightened. The government might now requisition empty buildings, barns and houses where regular barracks were scarce, thus making it impossible for His Majesty's troops to be quartered miles from the action as in Boston.

The Administration of Justice Act protected royal officials and soldiers by providing for their removal to England for trial if the Governor felt the colonial jury might be prejudiced.

Colonel Barré warned the House of Commons in vain that the Act was "big with evil consequences." The implication that a fair trial could not be had in the Bay Colony was bound to enrage the colonists, especially now when John Adams' masterly defense of Preston and his men was still fresh in their minds. The act became known as the "Murder Act."

"An Act for Better Regulating the Government of Massachusetts" was the crowning blow. The most precious rights guaranteed by Massachusetts' ancient charter, the "democratic part" of the government—that is, the town meetings and general assembly—were rendered virtually powerless. Now the Council, previously elected by the legislature, was to be appointed by the king. Several judgeships and other posts similarly would be filled by appointment from London. Perhaps the ministry only meant, as they claimed, to "enforce obedience to the laws." In fact, they destroyed free government in Massachusetts.

The Quebec Act, passed at the same time as the regulating acts, had no connection with them. It was a humane and tolerant attempt to deal decently with a foreign people under British rule. The predominantly French population was to retain its Catholic religion, its own legal code and social customs. At the same time, Quebec's borders were extended south to the Ohio and west to the Mississippi, a wilderness area no American colony would pay to administer though settlers were pouring into it.

Puritan New Englanders saw no virtue in the Quebec Act, considering it a threat to the "ancient free Protestant colonies" who, according to Sam Adams, should fear "Popery" above all else. The other colonies considered it a threat not only to their religion but to their hopes for westward expansion. In the minds of colonials, the Quebec Act was lumped together with the rest of Lord North's obnoxious gift package.

British legislators called the new brace of laws for the colonies "The Coercive Acts." The American colonists called them "Intolerable."

X

A NURSERY OF AMERICAN STATESMEN

> "... For abolishing the free System of English Laws in a neighboring Province..."

THE political communities that prepared to meet in a general congress in the summer of 1774 occupied only a narrow strip of land along the Atlantic edge of the North American continent. Pioneers, like Daniel Boone, who had pushed beyond the Rockies were too busy fighting off the Indians and mapping out new lands to concern themselves with politics. In June, Virginia's Royal Governor, the Earl of Dunmore, engaged Boone to conduct a party of surveyors to the Falls of the Ohio River, where he hoped to establish a "back colony."

In June, also, the Massachusetts legislature had sent out another circular letter calling for a meeting of colonial delegates to take place in September in Philadelphia. Rhode Island had already appointed its representatives, and by the end of July every colony except Georgia had followed suit. An Indian war was raging in that southernmost colony so the presence of British troops was essential to survival.

Only in Pennsylvania did the regularly constituted legislature select the delegates. In many colonies, the Committees of Correspondence in special conventions made the appointments. Delegates from Massachusetts' towns met in Salem to appoint representatives.

A "convention" of deputies from the Virginia counties resolved to send seven delegates to the congress. Peyton Randolph, the handsome and meticulous speaker of the House of Burgesses, was chosen to head the delegation, which represented the whole spectrum of political opinion and social status. Besides Randolph and the conservative soldier-farmer George Washington, there were the radical young men, the Lee brothers and Patrick Henry.

Each delegate was voted £90 for expenses. Portly Benjamin Harrison vowed he would have walked to Philadelphia rather than miss the congress.

Thomas Jefferson missed the meeting of the burgesses because he had become ill during the journey from his far western county of Albemarle. A set of resolutions he had drafted was sent ahead to be read by the delegates. His strong statement of principle took the position that Great Britain had no more political connection with the American colonies than had existed between England and Scotland before the union of those two countries. Jefferson declared that by emigrating, British colonials had negated all rights the parent country had over them. Only George Wythe, Jefferson's former teacher, agreed with this extreme position.

Virginia's delegation met at George Washington's estate on the Potomac on August 30 to travel north together. Washington's neighbor, George Mason, was there to warn them against a total boycott of trade with Great Britain. Without a market for tobacco, Virginia's economy would wither. Carolinians, too, needed Britain's market for their indigo and rice.

"To a redress of grievances" and "to peace" toasted the Virginians, raising their glasses of sparkling Madeira wine. The spacious dining room at Mount Vernon looked out over the broad Potomac toward Maryland. Soon the burgesses would embark by ferry to those strange northern provinces

A Nursery of American Statesmen

into which many had never before traveled. Suddenly the concerns of the "foreigners" to the north had become their own.

All over the colonies men were packing saddlebags or portmanteaus and boarding coaches or river boats for the journey to Philadelphia. Like the Virginians, many had never set foot outside their own colonies.

"I suppose you sent me there to school," John Adams said to Dr. Joseph Warren when he learned he had been chosen a delegate, "a school of political prophets, . . . a nursery of American statesmen."

Lessons began for the five Massachusetts delegates as they rattled southward over rutted dusty roads in a handsome coach with red and yellow wheels, loaned to them by patriot James Bowdoin. Committees of Correspondence from every town along the route came out to meet them. The trip through Connecticut and down the post road to New York was punctuated with excellent breakfasts and long dinners in the hospitable homes and inns of New England.

Only Robert Treat Paine had had much experience outside Massachusetts Bay. As far as anyone knew, Samuel Adams had never set foot outside Boston. He looked resplendent for the journey in a claret-colored suit given to him by the craftsmen of the Sons of Liberty. Golden buckles glinted on his shiny black shoes, and the gold head of his long cane bore the emblem of the Liberty boys.

The opportunity to become familiar with the people of different colonies and their way of life, opinions and fears worked two ways. New Yorkers, for instance, had replaced their Committee of Correspondence with a merchant-dominated Committee of Fifty-One. These leaders, John Adams discovered, were "intimidated lest the levelling spirit of the New England Colonies should propagate itself into New York."

Of New Yorkers, the straight-laced delegate from Massachusetts complained: "I have not seen one real gentleman, one well-bred Man since I came to town."

On down through Jersey the four chestnut horses drew their colorful coach. At Princetown (later Princeton) the Massachusetts men drank a glass of wine at the home of the Reverend Doctor John Witherspoon, President of the College of New Jersey. Though Witherspoon was a recent arrival from Scotland, John Adams considered him "as high a Son of Liberty as any man in America." With justifiable pride, the college president showed off the newly constructed planetarium to his Harvard visitors.

All the delegates who converged on the city of Philadelphia must have shared John Adams' sentiment. "There is a new and grand scene open before me. . . . I feel myself unequal to the business. A more extensive knowledge of the Realm, the Colonies, and of Commerce, as well as of Law and Policy, is necessary, than I am Master of."

Yet of the fifty-six men who drifted into Philadelphia toward the end of August—hot, dusty and fatigued—nearly all were experienced politicians. Each had been involved in his own colony's affairs throughout most of the decade of controversy with the royal government over colonial rights. Their combined education was equal, at least, to that of the Members of the House of Commons of Britain.

Twenty-two were lawyers, twelve of whom had been educated at the Inns of Court in London. The six American colleges were represented by alumni, Harvard leading with all five delegates from Massachusetts. Some representatives had been educated by tutors, while Judge Roger Sherman of Connecticut had taught himself law at his cobbler's bench. All but one had been born in America.

Nine had been delegates to the Stamp Act Congress. Thomas McKean and Caesar Rodney had then represented

A Nursery of American Statesmen

the "Three Lower Counties" of Pennsylvania, Newcastle, Kent and Sussex on Delaware, now a separate colony. The well-known Philadelphia lawyer John Dickinson and his colleague John Morton had represented the northern portion of Penn's grant. Together with Eliphalet Dyer of Connecticut, Philip Livingston of New York and Thomas Lynch, Christopher Gadsden and John Rutledge of South Carolina, they had made up one-third of the earlier Congress.

One elder statesman, Stephen Hopkins of Rhode Island, had attended the Albany Congress in 1754. The men in Quaker gray, the farmers and fishermen, looked askance at the high-nosed merchant and the wealthy southern planter, "all prinked out like a jibby horse in peach velvet and boots shining as if a cow had licked them."

"The Congress is such an assembly as never before came together, on a sudden, in any part of the world," recorded John Adams.

The staid Quaker metropolis put on its most festive air to greet its notable visitors. The bells of its many churches pealed a cacophonous welcome. The broad, tree-shaded streets paved with clean-swept brick seemed strange to men accustomed to meandering dirt roads. The mile-long stretch of busy wharves on the Delaware River, the buzzing countinghouses of the merchants, made the port of Boston and even New York seem countrified. Somehow the delegates dragged themselves from the wonders of the town and the pleasures of the many welcoming parties to settle down to business on September 5.

They had chosen the new Carpenter's Hall for their meetings over the Georgian majesty of the State House. Carpenter's Hall, built by master craftsmen for master craftsmen, was a gem of exquisite proportions finished with magnificent woodwork. Smaller and less convenient than the State House, it was free of all connection with the royal government. The choice seemed an unspoken pledge that this congress was concerned with artisans and laborers as well as merchants and landowners.

In the opening sessions the delegates agreed to call the group "The Congress" and the chairman, Peyton Randolph, "The President." These decisions were unanimous, but the choice of a secretary revealed a rift in the Congress between conservatives and radicals. Charles Thomson, the head of Pennsylvania's radical party and dubbed the "Sam Adams of Pennsylvania," was elected only after heated debate. Pennsylvania conservatives, led by lawyer Joseph Galloway, had successfully kept Thomson from becoming a delegate to the congress. His selection as secretary was an ominous portent to moderate congressmen.

The avowed purpose of the congress was reconciliation. Every colony's instructions to its delegates echoed those of New Hampshire, whose two representatives were first to present their credentials. They should, read Major Sullivan of Portsmouth in his dry New England twang, "devise, consult and adopt measures . . . to extricate the Colonies from their present difficulties; to secure and perpetuate their rights, liberties, and privileges, and to restore that peace, harmony, and mutual confidence which once happily subsisted between the parent country and her Colonies."

The method of voting, "whether it should be by Colonies, or by poll, or by Interests," triggered another lengthy debate. In the Stamp Act Congress the delegates had voted by colony, but Patrick Henry objected vigorously to following that precedent.

"Government is dissolved," insisted the persuasive redhead. He was dressed neatly, for once, in "Parson's gray," and his plea rang out like a preacher's call to salvation. "We are in a state of nature, sirs. The distinction between Virginians, Pennsylvanians, New Yorkers, and New Englanders, is no more. I am not a Virginian, but an American."

The words echoed those of Christopher Gadsden at the Stamp Act Congress, but now they set the delegates thinking beyond the immediate problem. Cautious John Jay had to remind the company that it was not the purpose of this congress to frame a new system of government, but to "correct the faults of the old one."

"The measure of arbitrary power is not full," declared the 31-year-old New York lawyer. "I think it must run over, before we undertake to frame a new constitution!"

The violence of the debate over voting methods prompted Thomas Cushing of Massachusetts to suggest that the members might work more harmoniously if they began each day with a prayer. The apparently innocuous suggestion set off another babble of dissent amongst that motley gathering of Episcopalians, Congregationalists, Quakers and a dozen other "fancy" religious sects. Though all were professed Christians, each group claimed that it could never join in the same act of worship.

In those first warm days of early September, while the members of the congress wrangled over minor questions of procedure, the tall, narrow-shouldered, broad-hipped figure of Colonel Washington could be seen talking to small groups out at the pump. With other delegates, he enjoyed long dinners at the homes of prominent Philadelphians, where "turtle, flummery, whip'd syllabubs and wines" were an exotic but regular fare. He searched the town's many shops for a riding chair for his mother. His friends knew that he would take no part in discussions until the petty quarreling had ceased.

Sam Adams' claret-colored suit became stained and rumpled, his fine white linen drooped. With the other, more radical delegates he endeavored to "keep out of sight" in the sessions, but nightly visited with small groups in the taverns or at private dinners.

The lovely young ladies of Philadelphia fascinated the men from less cosmopolitan areas. They minced along the pink brick sidewalks in wide-skirted dresses, carrying gaily colored parasols to match. Many affected the green silk masks, carried on sticks like lorgnettes, that were the rage in London and Paris.

The news that General Gage had bombarded Boston and that six people had been killed electrified Philadelphia.

"The bells toll muffled," wrote Silas Deane of Connecticut, "and the people run as in a case of extremity, they know not where nor why."

Congress was galvanized to action. Every member, dissenter or deist, joined piously in the prayers offered by an Episcopal clergyman, the Reverend Duché, at the opening of the September 7 session. The attack on Boston proved only a "Powder Alarm," but Congress was moving now. Two committees were appointed—one to prepare a statement of colonial rights and grievances, the other to review the many trade laws passed since 1763.

On September 17, sturdy, good-natured Paul Revere pounded into the brick courtyard of Carpenter's Hall with a new spur to action in his saddlebags—"the Resolves of the County of Suffolk," in which Boston was situated. The Resolves condemned the late acts of Parliament known as the Coercive Acts, declaring that "no obedience is due from this province" (Massachusetts Bay). They recommended that no taxes be collected until the government of the province be returned to "a constitutional basis," and they proposed a complete severance of trade with Britain.

The Suffolk Resolves still "cheerfully acknowledged the said George the Third to be our rightful sovereign." Diplomatically they bowed to "the wisdom and integrity of the Continental Congress."

At the same time, the citizens of Suffolk County served notice that they meant "to take all proper measures for our security," recommending that all the colonies arm themselves if only "to act upon the defensive."

The Suffolk Resolves were received with applause, even shouts of approval. "This day convinced me," John Adams recorded in his Journal, "that America will support the Massachusetts (Resolves) or perish with her."

Still the conservatives remained determined to adhere to their instructions which empowered them to do little more than "consult upon the present state of the colonies."

On September 28, Joseph Galloway, London-trained barrister and Speaker of Pennsylvania's Assembly, offered a carefully thought-out "Plan of Union with Great Britain." His idea that each colony should be a virtually autonomous state within the Empire, represented in a common council, was proposed ten days too late.

"We must come to terms with Great Britain," urged Galloway. "We want the aid, assistance and protection of the arm of our mother country."

Galloway's Plan of Union was tabled by a vote of six colonies to five. By rejecting it, the delegates in effect disavowed their instructions to seek reconciliation. On October 8, 1774, the Continental Congress approved the Suffolk Resolves, adding that, should Britain attempt to enforce the Coercive Acts, "all America ought to support them in their opposition."

So strong was the "violent" party that Galloway's Plan, along with the record of supporting votes, was stricken from the congressional record, giving the whole decision an aura of unanimity.

Six days later, on October 15, Congress adopted the

Declaration of Rights and Resolves. The committee assigned to draw up the document had labored on it a month before turning it over to John Adams with instructions to "produce something that will unite us." The difficulty was that the American colonies were following an uncharted path in rebelling against the rule of a parent country. How could they justify themselves? What, indeed, were their rights? And what authority did Parliament retain?

John Adams solved the dilemma simply by appealing to "the immutable laws of nature, the principles of the English constitution, and the several charters and compacts." The statement that emerged after some debate on the floor made clear that the colonists were defying Britain because their "rights, liberties, and immunities of free and natural-born subjects within the realm of England" had been violated.

The Declaration of Rights and Resolves was a faithful echo of a decade of colonial complaints, demanding the right of assembly and petition, the right to be tried "by peers of the vicinage" and the right to be free of a standing army in times of peace.

"They are entitled to a free and exclusive power of legislation in their several provincial legislatures. . . .

"But from the necessity of the case," the paper conceded, "we cheerfully consent to the regulation of our trade by Great Britain."

A series of "animated addresses" were sent off to the people of Britain, of the Province of Quebec and of the neighboring Provinces of St. John's, Newfoundland and Nova Scotia, as well as to East and West Florida.

A long letter to the American public exhorted them to accept the "mode of opposition recommended" by the Continental Congress.

Finally, an address to the king, written first by Patrick Henry, then softened and restrained by John Dickinson, was

First American editorial cartoon. Published May 9, 1754 in Benjamin Franklin's *Pennsylvania Gazette,* copied in 1775 by Paul Revere to dramatize the colonies' need for union against Britain. (Collection, *Library of Congress*)

Patriots fortifying Breed's Hill in Boston during the night of June 16, 1775. (Courtesy, *New York Public Library*)

King George III of Britain.
(Courtesy, *New York Public Library*)

Independence Hall, Philadelphia, in 1776.
(Courtesy, *New York Public Library*)

Committee of Second Continental Congress drafting the Declaration of Independence: Benjamin Franklin, Thomas Jefferson, John Adams, Robert R. Livingston, Roger Sherman.

(Courtesy, *New York Public Library*)

A Declaration by the Representatives of the UNITED STATES OF AMERICA, in General Congress assembled.

When in the course of human events it becomes necessary for one people to dissolve the political bands which have connected them with another, and to assume among the powers of the earth the separate and equal station to which the laws of nature & of nature's god entitle them, a decent respect to the opinions of mankind requires that they should declare the causes which impel them to the separation.

We hold these truths to be self-evident; that all men are created equal, that they are endowed by their creator with inherent & inalienable rights; that among these are life, liberty, & the pursuit of happiness; that to secure these rights, governments are instituted among men, deriving their just powers from the consent of the governed; that whenever any form of government becomes destructive of these ends, it is the right of the people to alter or to abolish it, & to institute new government, laying it's foundation on such principles & organising it's powers in such form, as to them shall seem most likely to effect their safety & happiness. prudence indeed will dictate that governments long established should not be changed for light & transient causes: and accordingly all experience hath shewn that mankind are more disposed to suffer while evils are sufferable, than to right themselves by abolishing the forms to which they are accustomed. but when a long train of abuses & usurpations [begun at a distinguished period &] pursuing invariably the same object, evinces a design to reduce them under absolute Despotism, it is their right, it is their duty, to throw off such government & to provide new guards for their future security. such has been the patient sufferance of these colonies; & such is now the necessity which constrains them to expunge their former systems of government. the history of the present king of Great Britain is a history of unremitting injuries and usurpations, among which appears no solitary fact to contradict the uniform tenor of the rest but all have in direct object the establishment of an absolute tyranny over these states. to prove this, let facts be submitted to a candid world, for the truth of which we pledge a faith yet unsullied by falsehood.

Thomas Jefferson's handwritten draft (corrected) of the first page of the Declaration of Independence.

(Collection, *Library of Congress*)

The lap desk on which Thomas Jefferson drafted the Declaration of Independence.
(Courtesy, *New York Public Library*)

Desk in Independence Hall, Philadelphia, on which the Declaration was signed, and the chairs used by the signers.
(Courtesy, *New York Public Library*)

The signing of the Declaration of Independence, July 4, 1776.
(Painting by Arthur Becher. From *The Story of the Declaration of Independence* by Mabel Mason Carlton and Henry Fisk Carlton. Courtesy, *Charles Scribner's Sons,* publishers)

Signatures of the representatives of the 13 colonies who signed the Declaration of Independence.

(Courtesy, *New York Public Library*)

Facsimile of the Declaration of Independence.

(Courtesy, *Historical Documents Co.*, Philadelphia)

approved. Holding to the pattern of blaming Parliament for all their troubles, the letter warned George III that "designing and dangerous men" were "daringly interposing themselves between your Royal person and your faithful subjects."

Reciting again the colonists' grievances, the address concluded: "These sentiments are extorted from hearts that much more willingly would bleed in Your Majesty's service..."

The Declaration of Rights, as well as the multitude of letters and petitions, had forced the representatives of the American people to spell out, for themselves as well as for Great Britain, just what they believed. On October 20, Congress backed up its words with the trusty weapon of total boycott of British trade.

A "Continental Association" was formed whereby the people of every colony "covenanted" together to sever commercial relations with Britain and to forego "every species of extravagance and dissipation." Associations within each colony would enforce the embargo on shipping, and "observe the conduct of all persons." Even merchants' ledgers and invoices might be examined.

Delegates from Virginia and South Carolina argued heatedly against the nonexportation agreement. Virginia pleaded for a two-year postponement to find new markets for its tobacco, while South Carolina demanded its chief products, indigo and rice, be exempted. The southern gentlemen walked out, returning only when Congress agreed to take rice off the banned list of exports.

On October 22, the First Continental Congress prepared to adjourn. They were resolved that, should no redress of grievances be forthcoming before May 10, 1775, another congress of all the colonies would convene at Philadelphia.

During the final sessions, each delegation prepared letters to its colonial agent in London telling of the activities and resolutions of the congress. Colonel Washington attended a farewell banquet at the City Tavern with the Adamses of Boston. There were many toasts and a mountain of Philadelphia baked oysters. Few felt they would meet again under similar circumstances. The delegates had unanimously expressed "the felt necessities of the times," and were optimistic that they would gain their objectives.

After formal adjournment on October 26, the Boston delegation started north.

"Took our departure in a very great rain," John Adams jotted in his diary as they jogged along. "It is not likely that I shall ever see this part of the world again."

John Dickinson was not so optimistic that reconciliation with Great Britain could be easily accomplished.

"Great Britain must relax or involve herself in a civil war," he wrote to a friend.

A new ministry that both British and Americans could trust was his hope.

Sitting alone in the assembly room of Carpenter's Hall, the "radical" Charles Thomson penned a note to his friend Dr. Benjamin Franklin, in London. He voiced the fears and hopes of every homebound delegate.

"Even yet the wound may be healed and peace and love restored. But we are on the brink of a precipice."

XI

LIBERTY OR DEATH

> *". . . For cutting off our Trade with all parts of the world . . ."*

WHEN the representatives from Massachusetts Bay returned to Boston in November of 1774, they found nine regiments of infantry spilling over the Common. Five companies of artillery occupied high ground like Fort Hill all around the town. There was even a mounted company of 400, the 17th Light Dragoons. All summer and fall, the transports had been bringing in the troops.

In the harbor were four ships of the line, HMS *Scarborough, Boyne, Somerset* and *Asia*, beside frigates and sloops and the numerous transports. From the warships, if need be, General Gage could commandeer 460 marines to bolster his already overwhelming armed force.

The Royal Navy ships were the only things afloat in Boston Harbor or the surrounding waters. A man might stand atop Beacon Hill with a spyglass all day long and search in vain for a merchant ship. Neither a ferry nor a barge could ply the waters around Boston except in the service of the king's troops.

Yet General Gage wrote incredulous ministers in London that all the king's men could not enforce the Regulation Act nor could the navy keep goods and food from flowing into blockaded Boston.

"Not a councilor or magistrate will dare act without a regiment at his heels," attested Lord Hugh Percy, Colonel of the Northumberland Fusiliers and second in command of the troops in Boston.

Governor Gage had moved his headquarters to Danvers, taking along a company of soldiers to guard the official residence. His thirty-six councillors, appointed by the king's writ of mandamus, were a special object of persecution. These well-intentioned Massachusetts Tories undoubtedly hoped to put a bad situation to rights. But midnight visits from the Sons of Liberty convinced many to join the patriots or to take refuge under the muskets of the king's troops.

Town meetings were held all over the colony in violation of the Regulation Act. To protest the appointment and payments of judges by royal decree, courts would not sit nor lawyers plead, nor would any jurors serve.

Boston shipmasters continued their business, sailing boldly in and out of Salem and Marblehead. Somehow goods and food found their way into Boston overland. Roads running inland were choked with carts, called by the country folk "Lord North's Coasters." Even fish had to be brought across the narrow neck at Roxbury.

Other carts, commandeered by the British for army use, were plagued with broken axles and wobbling wheels. Barges bringing hay for army horses sank mysteriously in deep water. There was no lumber for barracks, or labor to build them. Appeals for artisans sent out to other colonies were unanswered. Finally, in desperation, men were imported from Nova Scotia. Even they seemed annoyingly sympathetic with their Massachusetts colleagues, and the work dragged.

Though common soldiers slept outdoors, many officers found comfortable billets with the townfolk. A colonist was bound to give room, board, light and heat to a sergeant major or a regimental clerk when demanded to "Open in the King's name." Paul Revere's neighbor in North Square,

Liberty or Death

Francis Shaw, had a marine major billeted on him. Despite their prejudice against everything British, especially soldiers, both Shaw and Revere became fond of John Pitcairn, whom they found oddly gentle and understanding for a marine officer.

The summer and fall of 1774 were hot and frustrating to the troops stationed within the narrow pear-shaped peninsula of Boston. General Gage ordered company commanders to take the soldiers into the country for regular exercise marches. The regiments in their scarlet coats faced with blue or yellow, their white breeches and waistcoats and sabers flashing in the bright sunlight, were a brave sight. Small boys sat atop the stone walls that lined each route to watch silent and wide-eyed.

The soldiers, in turn, were amused at the antics of men and boys alike, who followed along behind or beside the line of march, imitating their every maneuver. Few noted the concentrated dedication with which the colonials drilled.

In every town and village throughout New England, militia companies and "alarm companies"—the home guard, made up of old men, boys, clergymen and magistrates—marched and countermarched. In Massachusetts the companies never disbanded after their annual muster in the late fall of 1774. So busy were the men of New England assuming a military posture that "the small game of the Province rejoiced in its sudden immunity from hunting."

A Committee of Public Safety, headed by John Hancock, was set up by the Provincial Congress of Massachusetts, meeting in defiance of the Regulation Act at Salem. The Committee was empowered to call out the militia "in a minute" whenever it was thought necessary.

That September, the British provided the Minutemen with a dress rehearsal. Without warning, a few companies swung into Cambridge, then Charlestown, to seize the province's stores of arms and powder. Immediately church bells tolled the alarm. Riders fanned out from the Boston area to spread the news all over the colony. In every town and hamlet, shopkeepers and lawyers deserted their clients, laborers threw down their tools. Overnight, thousands of armed citizens flowed into the offended towns.

"Though they had an account at Marlborough of the powder being removed, last Thursday night," wrote an eyewitness to the muster, "yet they were down to Cambridge by eight o'clock Fryday morning with a troop of horse and another of foot."

The men of Marlborough had armed and mounted themselves and covered a distance of thirty miles on foot and horseback in a matter of twelve hours.

"The colonists are numerous, worked up to a fury, and not a Boston rabble, but the freeholders and farmers of the country," General Gage wrote the Earl of Dartmouth, Secretary of State for the colonies. He urged a large army for the conquest of New England alone, predicting that Americans would fight well.

Despite the troops at his disposal, Gage dragged his feet. Loyalists called him a "lukewarm coward," while the British cabinet decided he was under the influence of his American wife and "too far gone to be recovered."

General Gage's warnings and news of the activities of the Continental Congress filtered into London during November 1774 in the midst of an electoral campaign.

In the streets and taverns of London, many Whigs and the more radical followers of John Wilkes backed the colonists. Bets were laid in St. James "that the American acts will be totally repealed by New Year's Day."

But the king's party won a fat majority in Commons. Thus bolstered, George chose to ignore the letters and petitions from his colonies. He decided that a resolute stand had to be taken.

"They seem to wish for England giving way to the opinions of North America," George wrote to his Prime Minister, Lord North. "The dye is now cast. The colonies must either submit or triumph. I do not wish to come to severer measures but we must not retreat."

Obediently, the government pronounced the New England colonies "in a state of rebellion," declaring that "blows must decide their status in the Empire." No one paid any heed to William Pitt, who pleaded that the troops be removed from Boston and that the assent of colonial assemblies be required for the levying of taxes.

"I say we must necessarily undo these violent oppressive acts," declared the aging statesman. He offered a plan of federation "lest the Kingdom be undone." The British Parliament rejected Pitt's proposal as decisively as the Continental Congress had voted down Galloway's plan.

In January, 1775, the London government ordered colonial governors to prevent, by any means whatever, the election of delegates to the second Continental Congress, scheduled to meet at Philadelphia that May.

". . . the first & essential step . . . would be to arrest and imprison the principal actors & abettors in the Provincial Congress (whose proceedings appear in every light to be acts of treason & rebellion)," wrote Dartmouth in an impatient letter to General Gage, whose dawdling infuriated the Secretary of State.

With his usual caution, the Royal Governor of Massachusetts kept the "Measure Secret" by simply not acting upon it.

Ten American provinces had already flaunted parliamentary rule by electing extralegal assemblies, composed mainly of men who had sat in the colonial assemblies. Every colony except Georgia and New York supported the "Continental Association" and set up local committees to enforce its Spartan provisions. Even in New York and Georgia, independent committees, facetiously dubbed "Committees for Tarring and Feathering," pried and poked in back alleys and hidden inlets to make certain no goods found a secret route to or from England and that no citizens indulged themselves in "expensive diversions and entertainments."

In every town, the Committees enforced the boycott and denounced traitors, and through them the patriots could exchanges ideas and formulate a program. Thus the Continental Association became the machinery of revolution and the embryo of a practical system of American government.

The first result of Association activities was a radical drop in imports from England that set merchants on both sides of the Atlantic to howling for relief. In the colonies, the Tories formed counter-associations to protect themselves and their businesses and property. Some members signed a pledge "to defend each other's life, liberty and property, and to support one another in the right to eat, drink, buy, sell, commune and act, what, with whom, and as they pleased, consistent with the laws of God and of the King."

Many loyal colonists—one of whom was Daniel Dulany of Maryland, who had protested earlier acts of Parliament, such as the stamp tax—now would have nothing to do with resistance that seemed already to verge on rebellion.

In New York, the popular Anglican minister, Samuel Seabury, in his "Letters of a Westchester Farmer," printed in *The Westchester Gazette,* called for disobedience of the nonimport, nonexport agreement. The embargo, he declared, would "alienate the affections of the people of Great Britain" as well as ruin the economy of the province.

By their resistance, individual Tories exposed themselves to the unbridled rage of the mob, while the verbal fury of the Whig press was unleashed against all the king's men. The organization of committees throughout the colonies continued at a furious pace. There were Committees of Safety, state committees, local committees. They threatened to assume control of all government powers. Taunted the Tory press:

> From garretts, cellars, rushing through the street,
> The newborn statesmen in Committee meet.

A Virginia loyalist took the matter more seriously, complaining that "everything is managed by committee, setting and pricing books, imprinting books, forcing some to sign scandalous concessions, and by such bullying conduct they expect to bring government to their own terms."

"If I must be enslaved," protested Dr. Seabury, "let it be by a KING at least, and not by a parcel of upstart lawless Committee-men. If I must be devoured, let me be devoured by the jaws of a lion, not gnawed to death by rats and vermin!"

An 18-year-old scholar at King's College undertook to reply to the venerable doctor's letters. With all youth's blind enthusiasm, young Alexander Hamilton stated in unforgettable terms the philosophy of the American patriots, while disregarding the sentiments of that other large segment of American people who valued their rights as dearly.

> The Sacred Rights of Mankind are not to be rummaged for among old parchments or musty records. They are written, as with a sunbeam, in the whole volume of human nature, by the Hand of the Divinity itself, and can never be erased or obscured by moral power.

The London government, meanwhile, blundering along under the illusion that discord centered mainly in Boston, offered a compromise tax plan calculated to pacify the other colonies and merchants on both sides of the Atlantic. In February, 1775, Lord North's compromise was agreed to by both houses of Parliament. It provided that any colony willing to tax itself voluntarily to meet imperial expenses was to be exempted from taxation by Parliament. The measure was an empty, meaningless gesture, doomed to failure, since it did not exempt the colonies from taxation, but made them, instead, the tax gatherers. At the same time, reinforcements were sent to stiffen Gage's wavering will. They were accompanied by three aggressive generals, Lord William Howe, Sir Henry Clinton and Sir John Burgoyne.

In March, Parliament passed the New England Restraining Act, forbidding the traders of that area to do business with any market outside the Empire. Even the fishermen were denied the right to fish off the Grand Banks. Justification for such stringent legislature was stated simply.

"As Americans refused to trade with this kingdom, it was but just that we should not suffer them to trade with any other nation."

Boston was already destitute. There were 7,000 unemployed in the closed port, almost half the total population. The idle dockworkers, sailors and fishermen milled aimlessly in Ship and Dock Streets, an ever-present threat to peace. General Gage set some to work clearing warehouses and wharfs, but the task seemed fruitless and the pay was negligible.

Prices of fuel and food were exorbitant. Deprived of any means to feed their families, many inhabitants were in a state of starvation. Few citizens could obtain wood to warm their homes.

Liberty or Death • *123*

During January and February, 1775, local militia in Portsmouth, New Hampshire, and at Salem stopped the king's troops from seizing their stores of powder and some brass fieldpieces. Early warning from Paul Revere and his circuit riders had enabled the townsmen to whisk powder and cannon to safe hiding places, "to prevent their falling into the hands of the King, or any of his servants."

British troops had withdrawn in the face of resistance. Gage was determined to avert bloodshed. But the Massachusetts Assembly was aroused by the threat of military force to appoint two general officers to take charge of defense preparations "until the Constitutional Army shall take the field."

Up and down America similar votes were being secured. In South Carolina a Secret Committee of Five was appointed in March to prepare the defenses of that colony. Soon they had supervised the seizure of the public powder in two magazines in Charleston, as well as the arms and stores in the State House.

Gradually the London government understood that the colonial unrest was by no means confined to Boston, or even the Bay Colony, or to a handful of soreheads and rabble-rousers. Acts to restrain the trade of all the colonies, similar to that applied to Massachusetts, were proposed in Parliament. New York alone would be excepted from disciplinary measures because it was considered to be loyalist in sympathy.

On March 22, 1775, Edmund Burke pleaded in Parliament for conciliation in the most memorable speech of his career. He spoke of the Americans' fierce love of liberty.

"The question is not whether their spirit deserves praise or blame," Burke declared, "but what, in the name of God, shall we do with it?" Burke asked for the repeal of the Boston

Port Bill and other acts in restraint of trade. He asked that the system of taxation be revamped. He hoped to influence the House not to "prosecute" the Americans as if they were criminals.

"The question is not whether you have a right to render your people miserable; but whether it is not your interest to make them happy."

The Irish prodigy spoke to an empty chamber. Most members showed their contempt for Burke's sentiments, if not his oratory, by staying away from the session.

Even as Burke made his plea, Virginians were holding an unauthorized convention in Old Saint John's Church, whose white spire rose above a greening hilltop in Richmond. Instantly, Patrick Henry took the floor to propose "that this Colony be immediately put into a posture of defense."

Excitement crackled through the gloomy church. Conservatives like Richard Bland angrily opposed the idea. Benjamin Harrison and Edmund Pendleton argued that the action was premature.

"How, Sir," asked Pendleton, "can our friends in Britain argue our cause if we show them we mean to fight?"

Patrick Henry, excited and emotional, swept away caution as decidedly as the House of Commons had ignored conciliation when he answered:

> Gentlemen may cry peace, peace. But there is no peace. The war is actually begun! The next gale that sweeps from the north will bring to our ears the clash of resounding arms! Our brethren are already in the field! Why stand we idle? ... Is life so dear, or peace so sweet, as to be purchased at the price of chains and slavery? Forbid it, Almighty God! I know not what course others may take; but as for me, give me liberty or give me death!

With the aid of former allies, George Washington, Thomas Jefferson and Richard Henry Lee, Henry's motion carried, though by a close vote: 65-60.

By April 5, the Massachusetts Provincial Congress, still hard at work developing defense plans for Massachusetts, adopted articles of war. Two days later the people were instructed to put their militia into a posture for war. Then the congress adjourned.

In the midst of this tension, Lord Dartmouth sent secret orders to General Gage, insisting that he pick up the ringleaders of rebellion. John Hancock and Samuel Adams, as well as Patrick Henry, were marked for prison in England and, doubtless, a traitor's death on the gallows. Hancock and Adams had already taken refuge with the former's kinsman, the Reverend Jonas Clark, in Lexington, twelve miles from Boston. There they planned to remain until time to depart for the Second Continental Congress in May.

General Gage decided to combine the expedition to pick them up with a raid on nearby Concord to confiscate military stores the patriots had been caching there since February. Some 700 troops under the command of Lieutenant-Colonel Francis Smith and the gentle marine Major Pitcairn, who boarded with Revere's neighbor in North Square, were ordered to move out of Boston on Tuesday night, April 18, "with the utmost expedition and secrecy to Concord."

XII

A HOUSE DIVIDED

"He has... ravaged our Coasts, burnt our towns..."

NO one knows who knocked on the door of Paul Revere's house in North Square the rainy night of April 18. The ruddy-faced silversmith was waiting for the summons. His North End vigilance committee had been keeping an eye on British troop movements all winter. During the past three days they had noted unusual activity.

Rowboats belonging to British naval ships had been hauled up for repairs and then launched on Saturday, April 15. This might not have caused suspicion but for the fact that the launching took place at midnight. The boats remained moored under the sterns of the men-of-war.

The patrol, alerted by the odd nocturnal activity in the harbor, was reminded that Gage's crack Grenadiers—the big heavy-duty troops—as well as the light infantry companies, fast, active troops used as flankers, had been detached from their regiments earlier in the day for some unspecified duty.

On Sunday, April 16, Revere rode out to Lexington to warn Sam Adams and John Hancock that trouble was brewing. On his way back to Boston, he arranged warning signals with confederates in Charlestown—lanterns to be shone from the steeple of Old North Church—one if the redcoats marched over Boston Neck, two if they left the peninsula by water.

At 10 P.M. on Tuesday, April 18, as Paul Revere hurried

A House Divided

along the dark cobbled streets toward the home of young Dr. Joseph Warren in fashionable Hanover Street, British troops were marching silently toward the beach opposite Cambridge. A barking dog was instantly killed with a bayonet. The soldiers were rowed across the narrow strip of water in longboats whose oars were muffled and dumped unceremoniously in the Cambridge marsh.

"After getting over the marsh," wrote Lieutenant John Barker of the King's Own Regiment later, "we were halted in a dirty road and stood there till two o'clock in the morning waiting for provisions, which most of the men threw away, having carried some with them. At two o'clock we began our march by wading through a very long ford up to our middles."

Twelve miles away, at 2 A.M. of April 17, 130 militiamen commanded by Captain John Parker lined up on Lexington Green in front of the Congregational Church. Shivering in the cold predawn, they waited awhile and then dispersed. Only seventy men reassembled at dawn, among them a free Negro, Prince Easterbrooks, and several Indians.

Meanwhile, the persistent tolling of the Lexington church bell had alerted the countryside. Three miles away in Woburn, 23-year-old Sylvanus Wood was awakened by the shrill sound. The sleepy youth decided "there was difficulty" there.

"I immediately arose, took my gun, and went in haste to Lexington," Sylvanus was to remember.

To the British Colonel Smith, leading his troops toward Lexington, the sharp tolling of the Lexington bell spelled trouble. He immediately sent back to Boston for reinforcements.

As the paling sky heralded the new day, Young Tom Willard stood in the window of Daniel Harrington's house across Lexington Green and watched the British soldiers marching up the road. A few brave birds trilled a greeting to the cold dawn of Wednesday, April 19, 1775. Later Willard recalled what he saw that morning:

"I, Thomas Rice Willard, of lawful age do testify and declare, that being in the house of Daniel Harrington, the 19th inst., I saw about four hundred of Regulars in one body coming up the road.

"As soon as said Regulars were against the east end of the meeting house, the commanding officers said something . . ."

(Major Pitcairn was warning his men, "On no account fire, or even attempt it without orders.")

"The Regulars ran till they came within eight or nine rods of the militia," continued Tom Willard's account, at which time the militia of Lexington dispersed.

"Directly after this, an officer hallooed after the militia . . . : 'Lay down your arms, damn you! Why don't you lay down your arms?'"

Sylvanus Wood, regaining his place in the line of minutemen, thought the officer then swung his sword and shouted "Fire!"

Musket shots rang out across Lexington Green. When the strong east wind had swept away the cloud of acrid gunsmoke that briefly shrouded the Common, it revealed wild disorder. Minutemen were dashing in every direction seeking the protection of trees and stone walls. Oblivious to Pitcairn's shouted orders, the redcoats pursued them with bayonets.

Jonas Parker, elderly cousin of the militia captain and trained in the grim school of Indian warfare, stood his ground. He tossed his hat to the ground and filled it with bullets, wadding and spare flint, ready for fast reloading. A British ball buckled his knees even as he tried to reload. A British bayonet finished him.

"The men were so wild they could hear no orders," the infuriated Major Pitcairn later insisted.

By the time Pitcairn regained control of his soldiers, eight Massachusetts men lay dead or wounded on the soft spring green at Lexington. War had begun, and independence from Great Britain—in the colony of Massachusetts Bay, at least—was a fact of life.

By the time the British force reached Concord, the body of militia that attacked them at North Bridge had quadrupled to 400 men. Here the British did indeed fire first, "the shot heard round the world." Two colonials and three British soldiers were killed, nine wounded, before the British began their disastrous retreat toward Boston.

Throughout the day, minutemen had been swarming in from the surrounding countryside, carrying the muskets that British law required them to own. Hiding behind walls and ridges that lined the road back to Boston, they turned it into a "bloody chute" for the redcoats. Although bolstered by Sir Hugh Percy, leading the Fifth Regiment, the British casualties reached 273. The Americans lost only 95 men. Thirty-five hundred colonials were involved in the engagement.

"Whoever looks upon them as an irregular mob," said one British officer, "will find himself mistaken."

Reports that swept the colonies and the world reached monstrous proportions. Both sides accused the other of firing the first shot. Each charged the other with ugly atrocities.

Two thousand militia remained encamped around Boston. On Thursday, April 20, a 16-year-old student from Andover recorded in his diary: "Early this morning we marched on to the common in Cambridge and expected the enemy upon us every moment. They did not come. . . . Nothing happened today."

Two days later, as the amateur soldiers started a ring

of siege works around Boston, the provincial congress met in an emergency session. It authorized the raising of 13,600 troops in Massachusetts, to be commanded by veteran Artemus Ward.

Meanwhile, in Virginia, the Royal Governor, Lord Dunmore, was alarmed by the growing number of militia on the march in every county. On April 20, he ordered his marines from the schooner *Magdalen,* moored in the James River, to carry off fifteen half barrels of powder from the round powderhouse on the green near Bruton Parish Church in Williamsburg. Angry men throughout Virginia prepared to march against the Governor. Patrick Henry led his militia from Hanover County. Within the week Lord Dunmore was "persuaded" to pay £230 for the powder.

Back in Lexington, Sam Adams had his hands full keeping his excitable young colleague, Hancock, from joining the army at Boston. The delegates to the Second Continental Congress were to remain in hiding until the end of April, when the five men were to depart for Philadelphia.

News of the battles at Lexington and Concord raced ahead of the representatives from Massachusetts. All along the route, they were greeted by crowds and bands and wildly pealing bells. The three Connecticut delegates joined them, and in New York, according to Silas Deane, they were greeted by an "amazing concourse of people." On across Jersey the eight men were escorted by militia companies and crowds of citizens. Before reaching Philadelphia, the New Jersey delegates joined the cavalcade, which was "met about six miles on this side the City by about two hundred of the principal gentlemen, on horseback, with their swords drawn." A Company of riflemen led the impressive procession into Philadelphia, where silent citizens lined the way and muffled church bells echoed through the town.

News of the battles in Massachusetts flew on south,

reaching Charleston, South Carolina, on May 8 and Savannah, Georgia, two days later. In that southern city, a Liberty Pole was erected, and Georgia officially allied herself with the radical cause by sending a token representative, Lyman Hall, from one parish, to the Congress in Philadelphia.

In the Virginia convention, alarmed by their own powder incident, cautious, conservative Richard Bland calmly proposed that Governor Dunmore be hanged!

He was not the only moderate shaken by the swift-moving events. John Dickinson wrote Arthur Lee in England on April 29:

> ... Why was not General Gage at least restrained from hostilities until the sense of another Congress should be collected? It was the determined resolution of some, already appointed Delegates for it, to have strained every nerve at that meeting to attempt bringing the unhappy dispute to terms of accommodation, safe for the colonies, and honourable and advantageous for our Mother Country ...
>
> But what topicks of reconciliation are now left for men who think as I do, to address our countrymen? To recommend reverence for the Monarch, or affection for the Mother Country? While we revere and love our Mother Country, her sword is opening our veins. . . .

When the forty-five delegates to the Second Continental Congress gathered in Philadelphia on May 10, 1775, the atmosphere was militant. John Morton, a gentle Quaker delegate from Philadelphia, confirmed Dickinson's fears that hope of reconciliation was remote. In a letter to a friend in England, he stated that the Congress was "preparing for the worst that can happen, viz. a Civil War. . . .

"Thou wilt hear before this reaches thee of the situation of General Gage. He is hem'd in by the Provincials. . . . You have declared the New England People Rebels, and the other Provinces Aiders and Abbettors. This is putting the Halter around our Necks, and we may as well die by the Sword as to be hang'd like Rebels."

All America seemed to be on the march. Everywhere, reported one citizen, "you see the inhabitants training, making firelocks, casting mortars, shells, and shot, and making salt-petre."

The Second Continental Congress convened in the Pennsylvania Assembly's first floor chamber in the State House, a more commodious meeting place than Carpenter's Hall. The king's arms hung over the main entrance of the plain brick building, with its squat wooden bell tower. But the bell itself bore a Biblical inscription that was to set the tone of the new congress:

> Proclaim liberty throughout all the land unto all the inhabitants thereof.

Most of the old members had returned. The new ones, in addition to John Hancock and the Georgia delegate, included revered old Dr. Benjamin Franklin, who had come back from England only four days before, as well as the able young Scottish lawyer from Carlisle in western Pennsylvania, James Wilson.

New York sent a larger delegation to the Second Congress, although loyalism was strong in that colony, especially in the upper classes and among the merchants and lawyers.

"When Conservatives realized that liberty could be won only by opening the floodgates to 'dirty democrats,'" wrote one contemporary, "many drew back in alarm; others, like John Jay, held their noses and carried on. . . ."

At least two of the five former delegates who did not return to this Congress, including Joseph Galloway, had decided their allegiance lay with the mother country. Within a few months they would be forced to take refuge within British lines.

The "military spirit" in the congress, of which John Adams wrote his wife, Abigail, was further inflamed by news that Fort Ticonderoga on Lake Champlain had been captured on the very night the delegates convened. John Brown arrived in Philadelphia from the far northern outpost on May 17 to report the story of the assault on the British stronghold. The highly irregular attack had been carried out by a Vermont border Captain, Ethan Allen, and his Green Mountain Boys.

Allen and his troops were considered outlaws by the colony of New York because they came from the Hampshire Grants, territory long in dispute. (Later it became the State of Vermont.) The seizure was somewhat legalized by the participation of a Connecticut militia officer, Benedict Arnold. In any case, the capture of Ticonderoga, along with two other posts on Lake Champlain, Crown Point and St. Johns, gave the colonials control of the important water passage from Canada. Cannons captured with the forts provided colonial forces with their first artillery.

The seizure of the forts forced upon the Congress problems whose solution its slim powers did not cover. No decision made at Philadelphia was binding on the colonies. Congress could advise but not demand, could recommend but not legislate.

"When fifty or sixty men have a constitution to form for a great empire," wrote John Adams, "at the same time they have a country of fifteen hundred miles extent to fortify, millions to arm and train, a naval power to begin, an extensive commerce to regulate, numerous tribes of Indians to negotiate with, a standing army of twenty-seven thousand men to raise, pay, victual, and officer, I shall really pity those fifty or sixty men."

"Our business has run away with us" was Silas Deane's dry comment.

The first step necessary, it seemed, was to take over the motley army already gathered outside Boston. On June 15, therefore, the Congress appointed George Washington, who had come to Philadelphia in his blue and buff uniform of the Virginia militia, to be commander-in-chief of the Continental Army. Artemus Ward of Massachusetts was to be second in command.

While these practical matters held the attention of the Congress, the people of Boston were being treated to a strange summer idyll. Since early June, British troops had been landing in the Massachusetts port. Thousands of soldiers were virtually trapped in the town, while General Gage observed the rebel militia digging fortifications on Breed's and Bunker Hills, twin eminences on Charlestown Peninsula north of Boston.

Fearful of being trapped, the British launched an offensive to seize the hills on June 17. Before dawn five thousand redcoats under the command of Major-General William Howe were ferried across the narrow river mouth to Charlestown Neck. The summer dawn revealed a vivid, terrible spectacle to watchers on the housetops of Boston and the surrounding hills.

Line on line of red-coated marching men assaulted the American position in frontal attacks up the hills. Twice they were repulsed. But as the New Englanders watched horrified, the British won the high ground while Charlestown flared in the background, set aflame by General Howe. The cost to them was enormous. The blood of 1,000 redcoats stained the hills. The Americans, defeated, won in the small cost to their men—139 killed, 36 missing and 278 wounded.

A postrider brought news of the battle to Philadelphia two days later as General Washington, with four adjutants, a troop of light horse and some militia, marched off to join the Continental Army at Boston.

"Oh that I were a soldier!" grieved John Adams as he watched them ride away to the strains of martial music.

The official report of the battle reached Congress at midnight, June 24. The next day John Adams had a more colorful account from his wife, Abigail, who was watching the battle from Penn's Hill near the farm in Braintree across Boston Bay to the south.

"Charlestown is laid in ashes," she wrote. "The battle began upon our intrenchments upon Bunker's Hill, Saturday morning about three o'clock, and has not ceased yet, and it is now three o'clock Sabbath afternoon. How many have fallen, we know not. The constant roar of the cannon is so distressing that we cannot eat, drink or sleep."

Four days later, Abigail wrote that they were being nourished on a diet of rumors. "We hear that the British troops destined for New York are all expected here; but we have got to the pass that a whole legion of them would not intimidate us. . . . We want powder, but, with the blessing of Heaven we fear them not."

George Washington, arriving in Boston, found that there was indeed no powder. Survivors of the battles at Bunker and Breed's Hills swore that the lack of it was the only reason for their capitulation to the British. There were few men able to serve and colonial defenses were poor. But the bravado of which Abigail Adams boasted was very real and a worry to the General. He wrote Richard Henry Lee:

". . . It is among the most difficult tasks I ever undertook in my life to induce these people to believe that there is, or can be, danger, till the bayonet is pushed at their breasts. . . ."

Congress, as well as General Washington, was fully

aware that it would take more than courage to defend colonial liberty.

At the end of June, sixty-nine articles of war for the "grand army of America" were approved. These consisted mainly of rather Puritanical rules concerning the moral conduct of the troops, urging, for instance, all officers and men "diligently to attend Divine Services." Many concessions were made to the general prejudice against military discipline but none to profanity or loose living.

Without a farthing of its own, the colonial assembly then addressed itself to the question of financing the new army. Since the colonies had no currency and no credit, it was resolved that paper money should be printed. Dr. Benjamin Franklin was appointed chairman of a committee to get copper plates engraved for the Continental bills.

Even while preparing for war, Congress was considering a second petition to the king presented by John Dickinson. On July 5, 1775, the "Olive Branch" petition was approved, so called because of its suppliant tone. It begged King George to intercede for his colonies in a designing Parliament. Governor Richard Penn agreed to present the petition to the king in person. Even Dickinson was doubtful of its success. He told a friend that if this humble application were rejected "with contempt," the British government will "confirm the minds of our countrymen, to endure all the misfortunes that may attend the contest."

The "Olive Branch" petition was followed on July 6 by a formal *Declaration of Causes of Taking-Up Arms,* authored by Dickinson with the aid of the newest member of the Congress, Thomas Jefferson, who had arrived in Philadelphia two days after Bunker Hill. The young lawyer's reputation as a penman had preceded him.

"Our Cause is just," declared this first Declaration. "Our Union is perfect . . . the arms we have been compelled by our enemies to assume, we will, with unabating firmness and perseverance, employ for the preservation of our liberties; being of one mind resolved to die Freemen rather than Slaves."

Jefferson explained his own feelings in a letter to a friend. "I would rather be in dependence on Great Britain, properly limited, than on any other nation on earth, or than on no nation. But . . . rather than submit to the rights of legislating for us assumed by the British parliament, and which late experience has shown they will so cruelly exercise, [I] would lend my hand to sink the whole island in the ocean. . . ."

A second *Address to the Inhabitants of Great Britain*, sanctioned on July 8, warned that victory over the colonies would not be easy. Then Congress again turned to domestic problems.

Three departments were created to administer Indian affairs. The Indians, still a constant menace on the western boundaries, were told to stay out of "a family quarrel between us and Old England."

On July 18 Committees of Safety in every colony were directed to take over the executive power within each colony and to superintend all matters necessary for each colony's security and defense. Many Royal Governors had followed Lord Dunmore's lead and fled to nearby ships and forts.

"We ought immediately to dissolve all Ministerial Tyrannies, and Custom Houses, set up Governments of our own . . . and open our ports to all Nations immediately," insisted the impatient John Adams.

But the heat of a Philadelphia summer was closing in, causing most of the delegates to yearn for the hills, the streams, the ocean breezes of home. They gathered more often in the nearby City Tavern to drink small beer and smoke long pipes. On the signposts near the entrance many stopped to read the handbills.

> To the SPINNERS in this city, the suburbs, and country.... Your services are now wanted to promote the AMERICAN MANUFACTORY....

Dr. Franklin chose mid-July to break his session-long silence, which had caused some delegates to whisper that he was a spy for the British rather than a friend. The aging Pennsylvanian, who had labored over fifteen years to fashion a workable colonial federation within the Empire, had reached an agonizing decision.

"I favor independence," the veteran statesman confided to loyalist Joseph Galloway and to his son William Franklin, Royal Governor of New Jersey.

On July 21, 1775, Benjamin Franklin placed before the Congress a *Plan of Confederation and Perpetual Union*. He knew the moderates were still strong enough to prevent his plan from even being mentioned in the congressional journals. Moreover, not a single colony had instructed its delegate to introduce the topic in Congress, let alone vote on it.

"The members can be turning the subject in their minds," the wily old doctor confided to John Adams.

Dr. Franklin was named to head an intercolonial postal system, and a plan for a military hospital was approved.

On July 31, Lord North's conciliatory proposal, already turned down by colonial assemblies, was rejected by the Continental Congress. In his report, Tom Jefferson ripped the veil of hypocrisy from Lord North's transparent attempt to trick the colonies into believing he was making a concession. His "proposition," declared Jefferson, "seems to have been held up to the world, to deceive it into a belief that there was nothing in dispute between us but the *mode* of levying taxes."

On August 2, "after the fatigue of many days," Congress adjourned for a well-earned rest. It was to reconvene in September. Despite the drama of the summer, the delegates remained divided.

"The Congress is not yet so much alarmed as it ought to be," regretted John Adams. "There are still hopes that the Ministry and Parliament will immediately receed as soon as they hear of the Battle of Lexington. I think they are much deceived."

XIII

INDEPENDENCE LIKE A TORRENT

"He has abdicated Government here, by declaring us out of his Protection and waging War against us."

INDEPENDENCE without government would be anarchy. Yet the governments by committee, set up in most of the colonies, were temporary affairs deriving authority from no one. They continued to profess loyalty to the king while resisting and even imprisoning the king's servants, firing on his soldiers and seizing his forts.

As early as May, 1775, Massachusetts begged the Continental Congress for "explicit advice" in regard to establishing a permanent civil government. The Bay Colony's legislators were most uneasy "at having an army established here without a civil power to provide for and control it."

New Hampshire, too, asked advice of the Congress, since her affairs were in a "convuls'd state." The Congress temporized. To approve a new government based on the authority of the people was to endorse, in effect, independence. Colonial leaders were instructed to erect governments only for the duration of the emergency.

Clearly someone had to grasp the reins of leadership, for the colonies were already aflame with civil war.

"To you they look for decision," Major General Charles Lee told General Washington.

Lee was a veteran of British campaigns. A newcomer to

Independence Like a Torrent

America, ancient, ugly, ill tempered and crippled with gout, he nevertheless had been appointed second Major-General under Washington because of his broad military experience.

The two officers gazed down on Boston from atop Prospect Hill in Cambridge. The city had been turned into an armed camp, with Tories from the surrounding countryside crowded into the narrow peninsula along with thousands of British troops. How long before they must burst out? The ragtag provincial army that hemmed them in was poorly armed. The hasty redoubts they had thrown up would be quite inadequate in the face of a determined assault. Defense was George Washington's first concern, yet General Lee counseled an aggressive stance.

"Your situation is such that the salvation of the whole depends on your striking, at certain crises, vigorous strokes, without previously communicating your intention."

Military necessity forced General Washington to take the initiative following the capture of the forts at Crown Point and Ticonderoga, which guarded the water route from Canada through Lake Champlain and the Hudson River. During the summer of 1775 word filtered back that the military governor of Canada intended to recapture the strategic forts and was even now "making preparations to invade these colonies and . . . instigating the Indian nations to take up the hatchet against them."

Canada's governor, Sir Guy Carleton, had only eight hundred regulars to protect his sprawling colony. In September, 1775, Congress approved Washington's plan for a swift offensive action against Canada before Carleton could be reinforced from London or Boston.

By mid-October, Washington had created a navy. His fleet of six ships, manned by New England fishermen and seagoing soldiers, was already harassing British supply ships and transports when Congress approved the general's action on November 25, 1775. Belatedly the lawmakers in Philadelphia drew up rules to govern the "Navy of the United Colonies."

General Washington disavowed the king's authority months before the colonies' cautious representatives in Philadelphia when he discovered that captured American officers were not being treated with proper respect. General Gage told Washington that he did not recognize their rank since it was "not derived from the King."

"The uncorrupted choice of a brave and free people is . . . the original fountain of power," replied General Washington.

He further encouraged independence in New Hampshire by authorizing General John Sullivan to seize all officers of the king as well as "that infernal crew of Tories," Americans who, he vowed, were "acting as enemies of their country." This was the first official definition of Tories and the first directive ordering their seizure. As a result, militant leaders in New Hampshire dared to call a constitutional convention to establish the first colonial government "by the people" and not by authority of the king.

Connecticut and Rhode Island already had liberal charters granting them the right to choose their own governors, but General Washington encouraged the idea of independence in other ways in these colonies. Knowing the army would back them up, Connecticut legislators produced the first series of laws directed against the Tories, whom Washington described as "preying upon the vitals of their country."

During the following month of November, Rhode Island leaders passed acts defining treason, and General Charles Lee toured the colony, forcing all suspected Tories to take an oath of loyalty. The appearance of a British warship in Newport Harbor doubtless inflamed the situation in that freedom-

Independence Like a Torrent

minded colony as did the shelling of Falmouth, Massachusetts' northernmost port (now Portland, Maine).

By the end of 1775 all New England was committed to independence. News from England that reached Philadelphia on November 9 set all but the most conservative congressmen thinking in the same direction.

A semi-official announcement in a Philadelphia paper on that day made it known that the "last dutiful petition to His Majesty" had been spurned. The same ship that carried that intelligence brought the king's official Proclamation of Rebellion, issued on August 23, the day before the "Olive Branch" petition even reached London.

The colonies were declared to be in "open and avowed rebellion," and all civil as well as military officers were instructed "to use their utmost Endeavours to withstand and suppress such Rebellion."

Americans were called upon "to disclose and make known all treasons and traitorous conspiracies which they shall know to be against us, our crown and dignity." In effect, the king denounced all acts of the Continental Congress as treason and those who obeyed such acts as traitors liable to the most severe punishment.

On October 26, in his opening speech to Parliament, the king asserted that "the rebellious war now being levied . . . is manifestly for the purpose of establishing an independent empire."

At the same time, George III authorized the raising of an army of twenty thousand troops to trounce the colonies into obedience. "Beating orders" were posted all over Britain calling for "all gentlemen volunteers . . . who are willing to serve their sovereign by saving their country."

The colonials could take little comfort in the rumors that few Britons would volunteer to fight their brethren across the sea. British officials simply looked around for foreign troops to hire. Six German princes produced 30,000 professional soldiers, peasants conscripted off the land for military service, for which the nobles received a tidy sum of £4,584,330.

This above all convinced the patriots they were outside the protection of their mother country. This final act of betrayal by England made America "fierce, frantic and invincible."

The "traitorous designs" with which the king charged rebel leaders were customarily punished by death. Far from retreating in the face of such threats, Congress replied on December 6 on a defiant note.

"Allegiance to Parliament? We never owed—we never owned it. Allegiance to our King? Our words have ever avowed it. . . ."

"In the name of the people of these United Colonies," Congress declared "that whatever punishment shall be inflicted upon any persons for . . . aiding or abetting the cause of American liberty, shall be retaliated in the same kind."

That winter was the coldest in years. The army that marched north in September, 1775, had been poorly clad for a winter campaign. They suffered cruel hardship on the frozen heights outside Quebec. Meanwhile, famine stalked the streets of provincial cities cut off from normal trade. Norfolk, Virginia's largest port, had been totally destroyed by bombardment from the cannons of twenty-four British warships. The New England fishing fleet was destitute. A smallpox epidemic swept unchecked across the troubled land.

A sense of urgency seized the men gathered at Philadelphia. John Adams saw his fellow delegates rapidly approaching the point of rebellion that he himself had reached two years earlier. Instead of exulting, he found himself "mourning in my heart all the day through."

Independence Like a Torrent

Outside Boston, colonial troops suffered through the chill autumn nights with insufficient blankets and food. Many men, discouraged, returned to their farms, especially as Christmas approached. As rapidly as a few disappeared, whole companies arrived from the south and west. They were the rifle companies authorized by Congress, and sharpshooters in buckskin from the frontier. Any one of the hardy colonists armed with a new rifled gun was worth a dozen British or Hessian regulars with old-fashioned smooth-bore muskets.

With magnificent defiance, General Washington raised the United Colonies' flag atop Prospect Hill on New Year's Day, 1776. The ensign of thirteen red and white stripes with British colors in the canton was in plain view of the British troops occupying Boston. At first they thought—hopefully—that it was a flag of surrender.

The port city was hardly a comfortable garrison. Loyalists from the countryside who had fled there for protection vied with their protectors for meager rations, housing and fuel. The Continental Army that ringed the city watched amazed as one Boston church steeple after another vanished from the skyline, the wood and shingles sacrificed for warmth. Even the liberty pole was cut down for firewood.

Meanwhile, General Washington was preparing a surprise party for the British garrison whose commanders never planned any action in winter. He had dispatched the former Boston bookshop owner Henry Knox, now Chief of Engineers, to fetch fifty cannons from Fort Ticonderoga. The heavy ordnance would have to be dismounted by hand, floated on scows the length of Lake George, then sledded across the snow-choked Berkshires—a seemingly impossible task. The fat and hearty Knox was undaunted. He wrote his chief in mid-December, 1775:

"Three days ago it was very uncertain whether we should

have gotten them [the big guns] until next spring, but now, please God, they must go. I have made forty-two exceeding strong sleds and have provided eighty yokes of oxen to draw them as far as Springfield [Massachusetts], where I shall get fresh cattle to carry them to camp. . . ."

Far to the south, in Philadelphia, the Congress of the Colonies was also bogged down in details of administering a country at war—a country that did not, in fact, exist. Idleness had never been a sin of these congressmen, but as more and more committees were created to take care of increasing business the working day became a measure of endurance. John Adams apologized to his beloved Abigail for not writing oftener, while Silas Deane of Connecticut wrote his wife:

"I rise at six, write until seven, dress and breakfast by eight, go to the Committee of Claims until ten, then in Congress till half past three or perhaps four; dine by five, and then go either to the committee of Secrecy or of Trade until nine; then sup and go to bed by eleven. . . ."

Congressmen were rudely catapulted from their routine on January 9, 1776, when a pamphlet titled *Common Sense* "burst from the press." Its reckless author denounced not only the British Parliament but the constitution and the monarchy as well.

Addressed to the
inhabitants
of
America
on the following interesting
Subjects

1) of the Origin & Design of Government in general with concise Remarks on the English Constitution
2) Of Monarchy & Hereditary Succession
3) Thoughts on the present State of American Affairs

4) Of the present Ability of America, with some miscellaneous Reflections

Philadelphia
Printed & Sold by R. Bell in 3rd Street
1776

Point by point, the daring penman ripped apart the fabric of traditional government.

"Society is produced by our wants, and government by our wickedness," the writer insisted, describing a primitive Eden in which natural law was corrupted by political codes. This natural law guaranteed the rights of man, not the British Constitution, which was declared "noble for the dark and slavish times in which it was erected" but now outmoded.

As for the institution of monarchy, "how a race of men came into the world so exalted above the rest is worth enquiring into."

The author saw "no single advantage that this continent can reap by being connected with Great Britain. . . . There is something absurd, in supposing a Continent to be perpetually governed by an island.

"TIS TIME TO PART! . . . O ye that love mankind! Ye that dare oppose not only the tyranny, but also the tyrant, stand forth!"

In an oddly mild understatement, Sam Adams declared that the pamphlet "has fretted some folks here more than a little."

Gentlemen who previously had mentioned independence only in whispers and behind closed doors now saw the idea blustered forth and defended in print. "As many as read, so many become converted," wrote one Philadelphian, "though perhaps an hour before . . . most violent against the least idea of independence."

There was intense speculation as to the identity of an author at once so rash and so reasonable. Even the sage of Congress, Dr. Franklin, was suspect. In fact it was the Englishman Tom Paine to whom the venerable statesman had given letters of introduction two years before in London. The son of a poor Quaker corset maker, Paine had failed in that trade and also as a shopkeeper and petty tax collector. Seeking a new life in America, Paine found immortality.

Ten days after the printer placed *Common Sense* in the bookstalls of Philadelphia, copies were being sold in Alexandria, Virginia. The pamphlet, said Edmund Randolph, "put a torch to combustibles which had been deposited by the different gusts of fury. . . .

"The public sentiment which a few weeks before had shuddered at the tremendous obstacles, with which independence was environed overleaped every barrier."

One hundred twenty thousand copies of *Common Sense* were sold within three months. Newspapers in America, Britain and Europe reprinted the whole text. Translated into German, it sowed the idea of rebellion amongst those immigrants to America who had found themselves so much better off than in their native Germany that independence had never occurred to them. It "works on the minds of those people amazingly," one Pennsylvanian commented. "This idea of an independence, tho' sometime abhorred, may possibly by degrees become so familiar as to be cherished."

Cherished or not, independence was becoming a fact of life increasingly more difficult to back away from. By February, Congress was considering opening the colonial ports to the world, thereby flouting all Britain's trade laws and regulations. The moderates fought a delaying action until February 27, when the harsh terms of the Prohibitory Act became known in Congress. Passed on December 22,

Independence Like a Torrent • 149

1775, it forbade "all manner of trade and commerce with the colonies." All colonial vessels were declared liable to "seizure and forfeiture." The Act left one small hope of reconciliation by empowering the crown to send commissioners to America to inquire into grievances and grant pardons.

But John Adams considered the Prohibitory Act an "Act of Independency."

> The King, Lords and Commons have united in sundering this country from that, I think forever. It is a complete Dismemberment of the British Empire. . . . [It] makes us independent in spite of our supplications and entreaties. . . .

Moderates in Congress were stunned into silence by the stringent measure. "Nothing is left now but to fight it out" said Joseph Hewes of North Carolina.

In Massachusetts, the fight had long since begun. Early in March, the colonial army took possession of the Dorchester Peninsula just south of Boston. Henry Knox had delivered the big guns from Fort Ticonderoga, and General Washington ordered them mounted on Dorchester Heights. They were cradled in bundles of hay, since the earth was too frozen to dig emplacements. Trees from neighboring orchards and barrels of dirt completed the fortifications. After three days and nights of bombardment, the surprised British, with a train of nervous loyalists in their wake, tried to quit Boston.

General Washington, watching the Tory exodus through his spyglass from atop Dorchester Heights, found little sympathy in his heart for the "wretched creatures." To him they must have appeared like so many ants trundling their worldly goods down to the waterfront in barrows, only to be forced to abandon them as the soldiers hustled them aboard the transports. Nature herself seemed to oppose their flight. No sooner were the miserable souls packed aboard ship than a violent storm whipped up the waters of Boston Bay, driving the vessels afoul one another and delaying departure for another day.

Eleven hundred refugees sailed with General William Howe when he decided to leave Boston. More soon followed —commissioners, custom officers, crown officials of every rank, as well as merchants, tradesmen, clergymen, farmers and mechanics and just plain "persons from the country." For differing reasons, they could not ride the tide of independence already nearing the flood.

Even the dismal news from Canada that the assault on Quebec had failed did nothing to stem the torrent. By April 6, when Congress declared the ports of America open to the world, it seemed obvious that the final break with Britain was unavoidable. Early in the year, Virginia had called a constitutional convention to create a new state government. Lord Dunmore, the Royal Governor, did his bit to hasten Virginia toward independence when he called on Virginians "to resort to the king's standard or be deemed traitors." At the same time, he offered freedom to all slaves who left their "rebel" masters.

James Madison, at 25 the youngest delegate to the state convention, felt this attempt to incite the slaves helped to push Virginia's moderates to the freedom side. A recent graduate from the University of New Jersey, Madison had been thoroughly imbued with a thirst for liberty by John Witherspoon, its president.

In March, South Carolina adopted a new constitution although its patriot leader, Christopher Gadsden, vowed he disliked the "indecent expressions of Paine." North Carolina swiftly followed and then, on April 12, became the first province to instruct its delegation in Congress "to concur with the delegates of other colonies in declaring independence and forming alliances."

Opposition to independence centered in the Middle Colonies—Pennsylvania, New York, Maryland and New Jersey. Pennsylvania was the crucial keystone in the arch of colonies that stretched from Florida to Nova Scotia. Yet the Quaker province's assembly, as well as its delegation to Congress, was overweighted with moderates like John Dickinson and James Wilson. While the colony's contribution to the war effort was unmatched, officially it still recognized the king's authority.

By mid-May, the whole question became academic. The majority of Congress was convinced that it was ridiculous "to swear allegiance to the power that is cutting our throats." Though Admiral Lord Richard Howe, brother of the General, had been sent to America with a peace proposal, its terms were no more conciliatory than had been Lord North's earlier proposition.

On May 15, the Virginia Convention, for which both Peyton Randolph and Patrick Henry had left Philadelphia, determined to force Congress to face up to the issue. Richard Henry Lee was authorized to present to Congress three resolutions "respecting independency."

On June 7, 1776, the senior delegate from Virginia presented his momentous resolutions.

> That these United Colonies are, and of a right ought to be, free and independent States, that they are absolved from all allegiance to the British Crown, and that all political connection between them and the State of Great Britain is, and ought to be, totally dissolved.
> That it is expedient forthwith to take the most effectual measures for forming foreign alliances.

> That a plan of confederation be prepared and transmitted to the respective Colonies for their consideration and approbation.

Outside the State House, the citizens of Philadelphia bustled about their daily affairs. Like most Americans, they had little interest in the deliberations of the Congress. In the endless wilderness to the north, where the province of Canada melted borderless into the rebellious colonies, General Benedict Arnold was struggling to get a remnant of his defeated army back to Fort Ticonderoga. The ordeal was a race against starvation, disease and harassment by hostile Indians.

For two days the Congressmen debated whether the time had come, after nearly two hundred years as colonies, to separate from Great Britain. Circumstances did not appear auspicious, yet most delegates received the motion as a foregone conclusion. No one spoke out flatly against it, although John Dickinson pleaded for a delay before the vote was taken.

"The people of the Middle Colonies are not yet ripe for bidding adieu to British connection, but they are fast ripening," he insisted.

On June 9, Congress moved to postpone discussion of independence for three weeks. Meanwhile, a committee was appointed to draw up a document justifying the act to the world. Three of its members, Benjamin Franklin, John Adams and Thomas Jefferson, had been among the earliest advocates of separation. Serving with them were Roger Sherman of Connecticut and Robert Livingston of New York.

Jefferson had received the most votes and so became, according to the custom of Congress, the committee chairman, responsible for drawing up the document. The Virginian did not need to look far for arguments to defend the American decision.

Jefferson felt no need to "invent new ideas altogether." Rather, he determined to "place before mankind the common sense of the subject." He labored diligently to make the Declaration of Independence "an expression of the American mind."

XIV

PHILADELPHIA, JULY 3, 1776

"When in the course of human events . . ."

ON Wednesday, July 3, 1776, Tom Jefferson felt he had awakened to a new world. He was now a citizen of the free and sovereign states of America!

On the previous evening the delegates from twelve colonies had voted for separation from Great Britain. This day the Second Continental Congress, meeting in Philadelphia, would consider the formal Declaration of Independence. Jefferson had labored over the wording of it for three weeks and mentally for months before that.

"And those political barbarians will probably pull it apart," Jefferson thought grimly as he shrugged into his coat. Every session of Congress was marked with lengthy, often petty debate. The colonies were split many ways—sectional, religious, political. Somehow they had to learn to pull together—or hang together—for all were traitors in the eyes of Britain.

But this morning Thomas Jefferson could feel only elation. As far as his declaration went, he had the firm support of his fellow committee members, John Adams, the Massachusetts fighting cock, and wily, aging Ben Franklin. Only one tiny finger of worry clutched at his heart as he gazed longingly out the window at the rolling pasture land beyond the city. Homesickness for the rugged Virginia hills surrounding his estate, Monticello, had sharpened since word had reached him that his beloved bride, Martha, was ill.

Selected Bibliography for Young Readers

Aldridge, Alfred, O., *Benjamin Franklin, Philosopher & Man*, J. P. Lippincott, New York, 1965.
Beach, Stewart, *Samuel Adams: The Fateful Years (1764-1776)*, Dodd, Mead & Co., New York, 1965.
Bowen, Catherine Drinker, *John Adams and the American Revolution*, Little, Brown, Boston, 1950.
Bowers, Claude, *The Young Jefferson*, Houghton, Mifflin Co., Boston, 1945.
Bridenbaugh, Carl, *Cities in Revolt—Urban Life in America (1743-1776)*, Alfred A. Knopf, New York, 1955.
Chidsey, Donald Barr, *July 4, 1776*, Crown Publishers, New York, 1958.
The Great Separation, Crown Publishers, New York, 1965.
Davidson, Marshall B., *Life in America* (a pictorial history in collaboration with the Metropolitan Museum), Houghton, Mifflin, Boston, 1951.
Forbes, Esther, *Paul Revere and the World He lived in*, Houghton, Mifflin, Boston, 1942.
Greene, Jack P. (ed.), *Settlements to Society*, A Documentary History of American Life, Vol. I, McGraw-Hill, New York, 1966.
Colonies to Nation, A Documentary History of American Life, Vol. II, McGraw-Hill, New York, 1966.
Hawke, David, *A Transaction of Free Men*, Scribner, New York, 1964.
The Colonial Experience, Bobbs-Merrill Co., Inc., New York, 1966.
Lancaster, Bruce, *From Lexington to Liberty*, Doubleday & Co., New York, 1955.
Malone, Dumas, *The Story of the Declaration of Independence*, Oxford University Press, 1954.
Morgan, Edmund S., *The Birth of the Republic (1763-1789)*, University of Chicago Press, 1956.

Philadelphia, July 3, 1776

The State House clock was just striking six when Jefferson turned into Chestnut Street. The city was already abustle. Industrious early risers, Philadelphians were customarily abroad at daybreak. An excited group had gathered near the narrow gateway in the brick wall surrounding the State House yard where newsboys were already hawking the early edition of the *Pennsylvania Gazette*.

"YESTERDAY THE CONTINENTAL CONGRESS DECLARED THE UNITED COLONIES FREE AND INDEPENDENT STATES" screamed the headlines.

Inside the State House, the colonial delegates were gathering in the long white-paneled assembly room with its tall recessed windows and brass-fitted fireplaces at each end. For over a year, the high-ceilinged chamber had echoed with the earnest, often angry debates of the patriot leaders pro and con independence from Great Britain. On June 7, only three weeks before, the resolutions concerning independency, presented by the senior delegate from Virginia, Richard Henry Lee, had all but split the cautious Congress asunder.

Now that the fateful vote had been taken, the members, who customarily met in committees before the regular session, were milling about nervously. Young Mr. Jefferson felt the tension as almost a living thing among them. The knot of apprehension inside him tightened as he moved toward the back of the chamber to find Dr. Benjamin Franklin. The veteran patriot was sitting tranquil and composed in his brown Quaker suit, chin resting atop his folded hands on his gold-headed cane. At seventy, Ben Franklin was the eldest member of the Assembly. For fifteen years he had woven his diplomatic way through the intricacies of British politics. He had felt the talons of the king's ministers and the scorn of his own countrymen when he tried to reconcile their views. Now he peered over his spectacles at the red-headed young member of the Congress.

"Cheer up," he said, as if reading the doubts behind Jefferson's lean freckled face. "You have written a fine paper. 'Tis destined to have a glorious life."

A nasal voice behind Jefferson concurred. "I am delighted, as I told you, with its high tone and flights of oratory."

Jefferson turned to look down on the domelike head of the rotund Yankee lawyer, who, with Franklin, had felt an immediate accord with the 33-year-old Virginian's draft of the Declaration. They had altered very few phrases, and John Adams had declared himself ready to fight for every word.

As Clerk Thomson droned through the day's dispatches —requests for aid, bills, committee reports—John Adams craned his short neck to see who was absent this fateful morning. The benches reserved for the New York delegates remained empty, he noted. With no instructions from their home assembly, they had abstained from yesterday's vote for independence.

Only five of Pennsylvania's seven delegates were present. Evidently Robert Morris and John Dickinson were still hoping for reconciliation with their king, but their absence on July second had swung Pennsylvania's vote into the independence column. Quaker Dickinson, a London-educated lawyer, though a staunch champion of colonial rights, backed away from any lasting rift with England. Dickinson could not bring himself to vote for independence, but John Adams had heard rumors that the peace-loving patriot had donned his colonel's uniform that very morning and marched his regiment to the aid of General Washington.

Washington, with his motley, ill-trained army bracing itself on Manhattan and Long Islands to repel the British invaders, was armed with little but determination. In his daily report to Congress, Washington had written, "I just now received an Espress from an Officer appointed to keep a look-out on Staten Island that forty-five ships arrived today, some say more, and I suppose the whole fleet will be within a day or two. I am hopeful before they are prepared to attack, that I shall get reinforcements."

Lord William Howe, whom General Washington had driven from Boston in March, was returning with reinforcements. The troopships he had gathered at Halifax formed the greatest armada yet seen by man. General Benedict Arnold was preparing an amphibious force at Crown Point, New York, to stop a British army under General John Burgoyne from sailing down Lake Champlain and the Hudson River to join Howe. At the same time, another British army led by General Henry Clinton threatened to overrun South Carolina. Even now British Navy ships were bombarding the wealthy port of Charleston, whose magnificent harbor could shelter the fleets of the world.

Thus, surrounded by the armies and fleets of the world's mightiest empire, the fifty-six men closeted in the assembly room at Philadelphia prepared to launch a new nation on the precarious road to independence. There was not a single wild-eyed fanatic among them. More than half were lawyers. There were four physicians and two clergymen. The rest were businessmen, plantation owners, masters of fleets of clipper ships—like the president of the assembly, John Hancock of Boston, the wealthiest man in America.

"And where is our hero of yesterday," wondered Adams, as his thoughts returned to the assembly room.

On the Delaware bench sat the gaunt stooped figure of Caesar Rodney. When John Adams had met him at the First Continental Congress he had thought him "the oddest looking man in the world. . . . He is tall, thin and slender as a reed, pale; his face is not bigger than a large apple, yet there is sense and fire, spirit, wit and humor in his countenance."

Now that countenance was shrouded by a green silk scarf to hide the ravages of cancer. Rodney had been absent throughout most of the session of the Second Congress. He had gone home to organize the Delaware Militia and remained there because of the intense pain of his affliction. With only two delegates present, little Delaware's vote would have split, one for independence, one against. When the resolutions were put to the vote, the independence delegate, Thomas McKean, had been forced to summon his suffering colleague.

On July 1, a wild storm broke the long hot spell. All night and the next day it rained. Booted and swathed in shawls, Caesar Rodney had ridden through that night and day from Dover to cast his vote for independence, thereby signing his own death warrant. For only in England could the well-to-do bachelor have obtained the required medical help to ease his agony or the type of surgery that might save his life.

The pounding of Hancock's gavel brought Adams' attention back to the matters at hand. He was surprised to hear the steeple clock ring noon.

"It is moved that we adjourn for one hour before taking up the formal declaration of independence that Mr. Jefferson of Virginia has drafted for our approval," announced President Hancock. Daintily he pulled a handkerchief from his exquisite lace cuff and wiped the perspiration from his forehead.

The room had become very warm, for the tall windows were open only a crack at the top to prevent the people gathered outside the hall from hearing the proceedings. The

Philadelphia, July 3, 1776

great oak doors were bolted against hotheaded loyalists.

The delegates rose to their feet and began to file out of the meeting room.

Thomas Jefferson did not join the rush for refreshment at the City Tavern on Second Street. He saw James Wilson, the young Scottish lawyer from Philadelphia, helping gouty Ben Franklin to his feet.

"We must hold our delegation together at all odds, Jamie," Jefferson heard Franklin say as the two walked off arm in arm. "We've wavered enough."

Out in the entrance hall, Sam Adams, rheumy-eyed and palsied, was a strange apparition in his red-lined cape. A bulldog when it came to liberty, old Sam worked unceasingly "out of doors" to bring foot-draggers around to independence. Now he was buttonholing delegates as they passed. Jefferson saw him slap Edward Rutledge on the back in a gesture of congratulations. The South Carolina delegate was, at 26, the youngest member of the Congress, as well as one of the most conservative. Yesterday he had surprised everyone by his vote for independence.

Tom Jefferson glanced up as someone touched his shoulder. His colleague from Massachusetts was smiling at him.

"Come along for a glass of stout," urged Adams, but Jefferson shook his head. He felt exhausted, drained—quite unsociable.

He wandered aimlessly into the State House yard to sit by the well in the warm sun. His thoughts still swirled around the declaration. True, the ideas were not new, but the hopes and studies of years had gone into it. Not only had he tried to present the causes of American rebellion "to a candid world." He wanted also to explain the new philosophy of government that, he felt, truly reflected the American mind.

Moodily he watched an Indian chief in his colorful tribal robes crossing the cobbled yard. Representatives of the Six Nations were living in a room of the State House awaiting the completion of the "Great Council."

"Strange," thought the Virginian, "that our pagan brothers can unite their tribes in a strong nation while we Christians, who pride ourselves on being civilized, argue and fight, and find it difficult to agree on anything."

Prompty at 1 P.M., President Hancock recalled the Congress into session, then graciously turned the meeting over to portly Benjamin Harrison. The elder delegate from Virginia had been elected chairman of the Committee of the Whole to consider the Declaration of Independence.

Mr. Harrison picked up the ink-stained, lined, already much corrected copy and began to read in a deep vibrant voice:

> A Declaration by the Representatives of the United States of America in Congress Assembled. . . .

"The United States of America!" It was the first time the title had been used in a public document. Chairman Harrison was not suitably moved. The handwriting was so spidery that he found himself wishing for a pair of Dr. Franklin's spectacles.

"If you please . . ." He passed the manuscript to Clerk Thomson to read.

At the back of the room, the author had drawn his copy from the lap desk fashioned for him by a fellow lodger at the home of Frederick Graaf. Now he eased back in his chair with a relieved sigh. Charles Thomson was an ex-teacher of Greek and Latin, a learned man with an excellent voice. He would do justice to the ringing phrases Jefferson had labored over into the hot June nights.

Philadelphia, July 3, 1776

The only sound was the buzzing of flies against the hot window panes as Mr. Thomson commenced.

> When in the Course of human events, it becomes necessary for one people to dissolve the political bands which have connected them with another, and to assume among the powers of the earth, the separate and equal station to which the Laws of Nature and of Nature's God entitle them, a decent respect to the opinions of mankind requires that they should declare the causes which impel them to the separation.

A murmur of approval rose from the Assembly. Mr. Jefferson turned a fine phrase. No changes yet.

The author glanced down at his own copy. Yes, this sounded better than his original, which had been altered slightly in committee. "To dissolve the political bands" had read—rather clumsily, Jefferson now thought—"advance from subordination," while the final word "separation" did sound more forceful than his original "change." He turned to smile gratefully at Dr. Franklin. The elderly gentleman appeared to be sleeping, his chin again resting, in characteristic pose, on hands folded atop his cane.

"We hold these truths to be self-evident," intoned the clerk, "that all men are created equal, . . ."

Behind his closed eyes, Benjamin Franklin was hearing and analyzing every word and phrase. He was glad he had persuaded his young colleague to substitute the simpler, more scientific phrase "self-evident" for "sacred and undeniable." Idealistic and high-sounding though Jefferson's phrasing might be, most of the delegates, and certainly the people they represented, were simple, straightforward folk.

"But on the whole, how brilliant yet precise this statements is," thought Franklin as Clerk Thomson began to read the interminable list of grievances against poor fuddled George III.

> The history of the present King of Great Britain is a history of repeated injuries and usurpations. . . . To prove this, let facts be submitted to a candid world. . . .
>
> He has dissolved Representative Houses repeatedly, for opposing with manly firmness his invasions on the rights of the people. . . .

As Clerk Thomson intoned the list of wrongs, an answering theme was evoked in the memory of every delegate. Each remembered personal indignities suffered for opposing "his invasions" on their rights.

> He has kept among us, in times of peace, Standing Armies without the Consent of our legislatures.
> For cutting off our Trade with all parts of the world:
> For imposing Taxes on us without our Consent:
> For depriving us . . . of Trial by jury . . . :
> For taking away our Charters, abolishing our most valuable Laws, and altering fundamentally the Forms of our Governments . . . :
> He has abdicated Government here by declaring us out of his Protection, and waging War against us. . . .
> He is at this time transporting large Armies of foreign Mercenaries to compleat the works of death, desolation and tyranny already begun. . . .

Words were added or changed here and there by members of the Congress to clarify or spell out specific points. There was little argument until the bitter passage denouncing that "assemblage of horrors," the traffic in African slaves. Into it Tom Jefferson had poured all the humanity of his fine, just soul. More realistic, both Adams and Franklin had been certain it could never pass this congress, but the author would not be persuaded to leave it out.

> . . . He has waged cruel war against human nature itself, violating its most sacred rights of life & liberty in the persons of a distant people who never offended him,

captivating & carrying them into slavery in another hemisphere, or to incur miserable death in their transportation thither. This ... is the warfare of the CHRISTIAN King of Great Britain, determined to keep open a market where MEN should be bought and sold. ...

"Objection! Objection!" Half the assembly was on its feet. The chair recognized the Reverend John Witherspoon of New Jersey. The Presbyterian minister was an outspoken opponent of slavery.

"But surely," he remonstrated, "the slave trade cannot be blamed on King George. The traffic existed long before he was born!"

"The issue is not germane to this discussion," insisted brash young Edward Rutledge of South Carolina.

Rutledge, like many another plantation owner in that company, was dependent on slave labor. Nor did the southerners alone feel an economic pinch in those dangerous phrases. Many a Yankee shipowner had made a fortune trading sugar and rum for Africans. Wealthy farmers in the middle colonies owned slaves, as did George Washington, even Thomas Jefferson himself.

"But freedom, sir, is a masquerade in a country that sells human beings in chains!" John Adams was on his feet, banging his hickory cane until the glass-prismed chandeliers danced.

His cousin Sam whispered to him as he sat down. "Do not argue over this passage, lest they take cause to alter other statements or, worse, turn down the whole."

Chairman Harrison was banging his gavel, trying to make himself heard above the angry voices. The closed chamber was stifling, though Jefferson noted at three o'clock that the temperature was only 76 degrees. The congressmen were sweating in their black nankeen suits. No breath of air came through the narrow openings at the top of the tall windows—only the pungent odor of the livery stable across Chestnut Street, and the flies. The fat black horseflies buzzed around the men's perspiring heads and nipped at their silk-stockinged legs. As the evening shadows lengthened, tempers grew shorter.

"Continue please!" shouted Chairman Harrison. "When we have heard the whole, we will vote on this passage."

> ... He is now exciting those very people to rise in arms among us, and to purchase that liberty of which *he* has deprived them. . . .

Here was the specter of slave rebellion, an ever-present nightmare.

"The King's friends who own plantations and slaves would suffer from such an uprising too," Rutledge pointed out. "That is our security. They will not take the risk."

As the discussion dragged on, President Hancock asked that the tapers lining each side of the chamber be lit. Their flames gave an air of gaiety to the room. The delegations had formed small groups for discussion. Oddly, the Virginians, who stood to lose as much as any from the abolition of slavery in the new nation, stood firmly with their spokesman.

"We should take up this matter when we are rested," Dr. Franklin whispered to Jefferson, who was surveying the commotion, silent and dour.

Dr. Franklin rose painfully to his feet. Sitting for long periods stiffened his gouty limbs. "I move we adjourn until tomorrow," he interjected. Somehow his voice was heard above the hubbub. The motion was quickly seconded.

"We shall reconvene Thursday, July 4, at 9 A.M.," intoned President Hancock.

John Adams hurried over to Jefferson, concerned at the angry flush on his long face.

Philadelphia, July 3, 1776

"Tomorrow will see it done, sir," he reassured his friend. "Come, let us escort our elder statesman to his chair."

After helping Dr. Franklin into his sedan chair, the two men strolled silently through the dusk toward their boarding houses. They made an ill-assorted pair. Adams was as short and round as Jefferson was tall and spare. The Yankee's rounded bald head gave him the aspect of an earnest gnome, while the Virginian's unruly mass of red hair stood out like a beacon atop his rangy frame.

Wholly different in background and temperament, they were as one in ideas and aspirations. Each understood without words the other's triumphs and disappointments of that day.

The two said goodnight in front of Frederick Graaf's fine brick home at the corner of Seventh and Market Streets. Back in his own barren little room in Mrs. Yard's boardinghouse, John Adams sat down to write his daily letter to his beloved wife, Abigail.

XV

JULY 4, 1776

"... We ... pledge ... our sacred Honor."

THURSDAY, July 4, dawned sparkling clear, cool for a midsummer morning. Just after 5:30 A.M., John Adams, always an early riser, was striding along Chestnut Street toward Joseph Vandergriff's tavern on the corner of Third Street. Every Monday and Thursday morning at six o'clock sharp, a stagecoach left the Sign of the Cross Keys for Princeton, New Jersey, a day's journey to the north. From there another stage would carry passengers and mail on to New York City while this one returned to Philadelphia.

Congressman Adams had several letters to dispatch, among them two for his wife, "dear Abby." He regarded Abigail's unfeminine interest in politics with amused tolerance, yet satisfied her curiosity with detailed narration of Congressional proceedings. The reserved little Yankee confided to her, besides, his most secret hopes and dreams for his country, as well as his opinions of fellow congressmen, too acid for other ears. He had written two letters yesterday, one in the early morning hours when he could not sleep because of the excitement of the vote taken July 2.

> The second day of July, 1776, will be the most memorable epocha in the history of America. I am apt to believe that it will be celebrated by succeeding generations as the great anniversary festival. It ought to be

July 4, 1776 • 167

>   commemorated as the day of deliverance, by solemn
>   acts of devotion to God Almighty. It ought to be solemn-
>   ized with pomp and parade, with shows, games, sports,
>   guns, bells, bonfires, and illuminations, from one end of
>   the continent to the other. . . .
>
>   I am well aware of the toil and blood and treasure
>   that it will cost us to maintain this Declaration and sup-
>   port and defend these states. Yet, through all the gloom,
>   I can see the rays of ravishing light and glory. I can see
>   that the end is more than worth all the means. And that
>   posterity will triumph in that day's transactions. . . .

Few Philadelphians shared the optimism of John Adams and other members of the Colonial Congress. News of the vote to sever ties with Britain had caused little rejoicing. The only parade John Adams saw this July 4 was the parade of wagons and carriages piled high with livestock, children and household goods heading out of town. Some said that the population of the handsome metropolis had fallen from near 30,000 to 21,000 in the past year.

The political unrest that had plagued the colonies for over ten years was worsened by financial depression. Many merchants, threatened with bankruptcy or by mobs of Liberty Boys, were moving west in search of new land and a chance to recoup their fortunes. Land was still the only real wealth in North America except for Spanish gold doubloons. On May 22, Congress had authorized the printing of dollars to stabilize the many different species used in the colonies, but none were yet in circulation. Most citizens would think the paper currency worthless anyway.

But this morning John Adams surmised it was fear of the British that sent folks scurrying to the hills. The stagecoach was nearly empty of passengers, and those few would not venture farther than Princeton, he was told.

"Now don't send these letters into New York City, Eb,"

Adams warned the coach driver. "I wouldn't want the British to get hold of them."

"Count on me, sir," the driver assured the portly congressman. "I'll see 'em in the hands of the postrider meself, like always."

General Washington's Colonials occupied the city of New York, but the area was crawling with Tories, while British troops probably were landing at this very moment. Postriders could bypass the city by riding up the west side of the Hudson River, crossing at Dobb's Ferry or Tarrytown, thence east and north to Connecticut and Massachusetts.

An exhausted rider was stabling his horse as John Adams approached the State House. He had brought yesterday's dispatches from General Washington to Congress. The situation had worsened. On July 3, over 9,000 British troops had landed on Staten Island. Washington felt certain that Lord Howe planned to surround the city. Congress' first order of the day that July 4 was to find new supplies of flints for the armies on Manhattan and Long Islands.

By 1 P.M. it was again a sticky 76 degrees in the council chamber, the air unmoving. The tall windows remained closed and shaded against the sun. The buzzing of the ever-present flies droned a monotonous accompaniment to Clerk Thomson's rereading of the Declaration of Independence.

Benjamin Franklin found his eyes attracted to the wall behind President Hancock's desk, where fingers of sunlight glinted on the panoply of British drums, swords and banners. They had been captured at Fort Ticonderoga the year before by Colonel Benedict Arnold, with Ethan Allen and his Green Mountain boys—"in the name of the great Jehovah and the Continental Congress."

"Neither of which had given such authority," thought Dr. Franklin wryly. "But I hope the latter will have the power to do so after today."

July 4, 1776

Painfully Franklin turned to see how his young neighbor was reacting to this second reading of his document. Jefferson's long face seemed more gaunt and pallid than usual, but he appeared relaxed as he made notations and corrections on his own draft of the Declaration. Nearby, John Adams was whispering urgently into the attentive ear of his elderly relative, Sam. Young Abraham Clark of New Jersey was scribbling a letter.

New Jersey had sent a new delegation in mid-June when that colony unseated its Royal Governor and Council. Franklin had special reason to be interested, since the deposed governor was his own son, William. Led by the learned President of Princeton University, Dr. Witherspoon, all four representatives of the new group were "high-charged with independence."

Dr. Franklin was startled from his reverie by the spectacle of that dignified Scottish minister leaping to his feet, red-faced, hands waving. He appeared to have lost the power of speech.

"I must have missed something important," thought Franklin and turned to ask his colleague, Jamie Wilson, only to find him on his feet too. The lawyer, also a Scot, was trembling with rage, his face a splotchy red as though he had been slapped.

Taking Wilson's arm and leaning heavily on his knobby cane, Dr. Franklin struggled to his feet. So seldom did he speak in assembly that he was immediately the focus of all eyes.

"Mr. Chairman," he called, "I am afraid my aging ears have missed some of the reading. If you would favor an ailing old man by repeating . . ."

The ridiculous and exaggerated picture Dr. Franklin drew of himself afforded the chamber a much-needed chuckle. The veteran politician pulled his young friend down beside him.

"They're coupling us Scots with those blasphemous German fellows," Wilson stammered.

Clerk Thomson reread the passage in question:

> Nor have we been wanting in attentions to our British brethren. . . .
> We have reminded them of the circumstances of our emigration and settlement here. . . . They too have been deaf to the voice of justice and consanguity. . . . At this very time too, they are permitting their chief magistrate to send over . . . Scotch and foreign mercenaries to invade and destroy us. . . .

More than half of Jefferson's bitter tirade had already been deleted. The author's hair was damp, and his long face dour with disapproval as the Chairman struck out line after line.

" 'Tis the term 'Scotch and other foreign mercenaries" I resent," Dr. Witherspoon announced, having regained his usual calm.

"I move it be stricken," added Wilson.

No one disputed the two Scottish-born delegates. Chairman Harrison ordered the clerk to read on.

> These facts have given the last stab to agonizing affection, and manly spirit bids us renounce forever these unfeeling brethren. . . . We must forget our former love for them. . . . We might have a free and great people together, but a communication of grandeur and of freedom, it seems, is below their dignity. Be it so. . . . We will tread . . . apart from them and acquiesce in the necessity which denounces our eternal separation. . . .

Throughout the reading of this passage, a number of delegates had been shaking their heads. Now there was a roar of protest. The words "forever" and "eternal" had to go.

"Many of our British brethren have plead our cause," someone reminded the assembly. "They have been faithful to the ties of blood and mindful of our rights as freeborn Englishmen. Surely it were folly to sever relations forever!"

"Our quarrel is with the King and his ministers..."

"We may have to deal with Parliament someday..."

So through the muggy afternoon the men trimmed and refined the instrument of their rebellion. The author of the document found his mind wandering. Through the window, he could just see the top of Philadelphia's planetarium. The course of the heavenly bodies, mused Jefferson, is certainly more restful and more predictable than Congress in action. But these were the birth pangs of a new nation, he reminded himself, and the labor had only just begun.

He found himself thinking of his Virginia neighbor. George Washington would soon face his bitterest test. He was to oppose in battle those very officers and soldiers beside whom he had so recently fought against the Indians and French. Washington would stand firm as the Blue Ridge Mountains.

"We must, therefore, acquiesce in the necessity, which denounces our Separation," Clerk Thomson was reading the revised version, "and hold them, as we hold the rest of mankind, Enemies in War, in Peace Friends."

Jefferson was drained of anger, though he realized that almost the whole last paragraph had been deleted.

Now several delegates suggested that the final paragraph be amended to include the wording of the Virginia Resolves presented by Richard Henry Lee and voted upon July 2.

"For was it not with the acceptance of those resolutions that we made the break and became independent states?" Edward Rutledge pointed out.

Before the vote could be taken, a decision, they were reminded, had to be reached on the controversial slavery passage. Though most of the delegates opposed slavery in principle, Carolina and Georgia stood firm against including the passage in the Declaration.

"Everyone knows that Roman law, a model of justice, recognized slavery as a legal institution," pointed out Arthur Middleton, a Carolina representative who was seldom heard from because he always had his nose in some classical tome.

"If left alone, slavery in Georgia will be gradually ended," assured one Georgian.

John Adams fidgeted impatiently as his great gold pocket watch ticked away the precious minutes. The Declaration, he thought must go through before some unforeseen event canceled all their efforts for independence. Much as he abhorred slavery, he knew the issue must be sacrificed to the more immediate cause. He looked meaningfully at his cousin Sam, who immediately indicated he wished to make a motion.

"I move that all matters pertaining to the situation of our black brethren be expunged from the document," Sam Adams stated clearly.

"Hear. Hear!" Several voices seconded the motion.

> We, therefore, the representatives of the United States of America in General Congress, . . .

Clerk Thomson continued the reading in a proud ringing voice, as the whole chamber fell silent.

> . . . appealing to the Supreme Judge of the world for the rectitude of our intentions, do, in the Name, and by the authority of the good People of these Colonies, solemnly publish and declare, That these United Colonies are, and of Right ought to be FREE AND INDEPENDENT STATES; that they are Absolved from all

July 4, 1776 • 173

> Allegiance to the British Crown, and that all political connection between them and the State of Great Britain is, and ought to be totally dissolved; . . .

Abraham Clark was so filled with emotion that he felt he must have an outlet or burst. Seizing the pen he had laid aside during the discussions, he resumed his letter writing.

"We are now embarked on a most tempestuous sea," he confided to his friend Elias Drayton. "Congress may soon be exalted on a high gallows. Let us prepare for the worst, we can die but once."

Clark's mood was mirrored around the room. Most of the delegates were on their feet when the clerk reached the final phrases.

> And for the support of this Declaration, with a firm reliance on the protection of divine Providence, we mutually pledge to each other our Lives, our Fortunes, and our Sacred Honor.

For a moment there was no sound. The whole assembly remained standing together as if to solemnize the pledge. Indeed they now had only divine providence and each other on which to depend, for they had renounced their king and country. There were many battles yet to be fought, a nation to be forged out of thirteen diverse and quarrelsome colonies. Each remembered friends and family. If they were in America, would the action taken in Philadelphia today help or harm them? If they were still in England, would they ever meet again?

And if the independence movement failed? This Declaration would be their passport to the gallows. Their homes would be burned, their land and livestock confiscated, their wives and children disgraced.

The silence was broken by the positive voice of the committee chairman.

"There, sir, is your Declaration," boomed Benjamin Harrison, handing the lined and sweat-stained paper to President Hancock. "If the Committee of the Whole House will signify that they accept this document, I will turn the meeting back to you."

"Aye," fifty-five voices replied in unanimous assent.

John Hancock flipped back his lace cuffs and picked up the quill pen from the speaker's table. With a regal flourish the President of Congress dipped the quill into the heavy silver inkstand. "If Clerk Thomson will witness . . ."

John Hancock signed the Declaration of Independence in fine bold script.

"His Majesty can read my name without his glasses," explained the Boston merchant, "and can double the reward on my head." Since before the Battle at Lexington there had been a reward of five hundred pounds for Hancock's arrest.

When Thomson had signed as witness, there was a discussion as to how the document was to be authenticated. The King's great seal had always been used for official documents. It was moved that a committee be formed to secure a device to be used as a seal. Dr. Franklin, John Adams and Thomas Jefferson were charged with this further duty.

The mutilated copy of the Declaration was returned to the author to be printed.

"Copies must be sent to the several assemblies for ratification," reminded Hancock, "and to the several commanders of the continental troops. The Declaration must be proclaimed throughout the United States and read out to the armies. We must have, besides, a copy embossed on parchment to be signed by every member of this assembly. For security reasons, the names of those present must be kept secret until that time. So record it in the Secret Journal," the President ordered.

It was late evening before the Congress of the new

United States adjourned. They would resume business as usual early the next morning, July 5. While most of the delegates sought food and ale, Jefferson hurried directly to the printer's shop. The man would have to work most of the night to set the type for the broadsides to be sent out tomorrow.

John Adams was not hungry. He walked through the cooling summer dusk, thoughts whirling excitedly in his head.

"When I look back to the year 1761," he had written to Abby the previous night, "and recollect the argument concerning writs of assistance in the superior court, which I have hitherto considered as the commencement of this controversy between Great Britain and America, and run through the whole period from that time to this, and recollect the series of political events, the chain of causes and effects, I am surprised at the suddenness as well as greatness of this revolution. . . ."

EPILOGUE

ON Monday, July 8, 1776, *A Declaration by the Representatives of the United States in General Congress Assembled* was read in the State House yard at Philadelphia. Mr. John Nixon, a member of the Committee of Safety, intoned Thomas Jefferson's ringing phrases concerning the God-given and unalienable rights of men. He stood atop an ugly wooden platform erected some years before by the American Philosophical Society for the observation of stars.

A broiling sun beat down on the listening throng that filled the yard and spilled through the one opening in the high stone wall to spread over Walnut Street. The people listened silently until the reader began the long list of "injuries and usurpations" inflicted by "the present King of Great Britain" on his subjects in the American colonies. Each of these was greeted with a roar.

The final declaration that "these united colonies are, and of right ought to be, free and independent states" brought "three repeated huzzas." Church bells began to toll, continuing throughout the day and night while citizens paraded in the streets. In the evening the taverns overflowed. Bonfires blazed and, despite the critical shortage of gunpowder, salutes were fired with muskets and cannons left over from the French wars and some new "Kentucky" rifles that were actually manufactured in Pennsylvania.

Epilogue

Similar scenes occurred that day in Easton, Pennsylvania, and in Trenton, New Jersey.

At 6 P.M. on Tuesday, July 9, General George Washington mustered the militia under his command in the city of New York to hear the proclamation. Lined up near the Battery, the soldiers greeted the Declaration with cheers that might well have been heard by British troops still aboard ships in the lower bay off Staten Island.

That same evening, the New York colonial convention was in session some miles to the north in the courthouse at White Plains. Till then split on the independence issue, they decided that evening that Congress's reasons for declaring the colonies free and independent states were "cogent and conclusive." New instructions were posted to the New York delegates at Philadelphia.

The "Unanimous Declaration of the Thirteen United States of America" was read in towns and militia camps throughout the country during the month of July and into August. Each public reading was heralded with cheers, ringing bells and bonfires. Gallons of rum and wine were consumed in countless toasts. Liberty poles were erected, and George III was burned in effigy again and again. Pounds of precious gunpowder were wasted in salutes.

Loyalists watched the celebrations from behind closed shutters, for the Declaration of Independence was by no means unanimously accepted. One Tory vowed that "a more impudent, false and atrocious Proclamation was never fabricated by the hands of man."

"The Declaration of Independency is variously relished here," wrote Alexander Graydon of Worcester, Massachusetts. "However, the matter is now settled and our salvation depends upon supporting the measure."

Overseas the reaction to the Declaration ranged from the horror of many British to the admiration of the French.

At the instigation of the English Cabinet, John Lind published "An Answer to the Declaration of the American Congress" with this indictment: "They have put the axe to the root of all government . . . some one or other of these rights pretended to be unalienable, is actually alienated" in all governments.

On the other hand, Condorcet, the great French philosopher and close friend of Benjamin Franklin, recognized its greatness immediately: "The act which declares [America's] independence is a simple and sublime exposition of those rights so sacred and long forgotten."

The Abbé Galiani wrote a friend in Paris in 1776 that the age is one of "the total fall of Europe, and of transmigration into America." In the New World, he declared, law, religion, science and the arts would renew themselves. "Therefore," advised the practical Abbé, "do not buy your house in the Chausée d'Antin; you must buy it in Philadelphia."

On January 31, 1777, with the Declaration six months old, John Hancock sent a circular letter to each of the states with a copy of the document enclosed. He wrote: "The Memory of that Transaction, together with the Causes that gave rise to it, should be preserved in the most careful Manner that can be devised . . . it may henceforth form a Part of the Archives of your State. . . ."

The original parchment had traveled far since its presentation in Philadelphia. As Congress moved, it was carried along with the other records. When George Washington was inaugurated President of the United States in 1789, the Secretary of the Congress delivered the document to him in New York. It was placed in the custody of the Secretary of State from the time that office was created. With perfect symbolism, our first Secretary of State was Thomas Jefferson.

Epilogue

The DECLARATION OF INDEPENDENCE is today a yellowing parchment housed in a tomblike vehicle in the National Archives at Washington, D. C.* At 10 P.M. each evening, a guard presses a button that lowers it for safekeeping to the cavernous basement by means of an electric elevator device. Each morning it is raised again into its glass and metal case to be viewed by the thousands of adults and children who troop through the vast lobby each day.

For even the brightest young eyes, the crablike script in which the Declaration is written is almost illegible. Most of the measured phrases are of little interest today, circumscribed as they are by the political events of nearly 200 years ago.

The Preamble, which remains of abiding interest, slipped past the censorious pencil of the conservative Founding Fathers almost by accident. Perhaps they thought Tom Jefferson's ringing phrases about all men being created equal were too general in tone to cause trouble or concern.

Yet these very "glittering and high-sounding generalities" distilled into words the best political thinking of the eighteenth century, sounding the tocsin of a new world order. The echo of those phrases still reverberates across the world.

John Adams had said that the revolution was in the hearts and minds of men, and there it remains. Every generation of Americans has signed the Declaration with its blood. And still we hold these truths to be self-evident.

Did those beleaguered patriots, sweltering in the humid heat of a Philadelphia summer, threatened by the mighty arms of the very nation to whom some still felt a lingering allegiance, uncertain of their support at home or even of the

---

* A part of Jefferson's original draft, showing changes and corrections, may be found in the Library of Congress, Washington, D. C.

rightness of their course, have any conception of the full impact of their Declaration on generations to come?

Surely not. Yet the words of some, like Washington, Adams, Franklin and Jefferson, seem to indicate, they did know and understood fully what they were doing. As poet Robert Frost has so beautifully stated:

> So much those heroes knew and understood . . .
> They must have seen ahead what now appears,
> They would bring empires down about our ears
> And by the example of our Declaration
> Make everybody want to be a nation.

THE DECLARATION OF INDEPENDENCE

In Congress, July 4, 1776

The Unanimous Declaration of the Thirteen United States of America

When in the course of human events, it becomes necessary for one people to dissolve the political bands which have connected them with another, and to assume among the powers of the earth, the separate and equal station to which the Laws of Nature and of Nature's God entitle them, a decent respect to the opinions of mankind requires that they should declare the causes which impel them to the separation.

We hold these truths to be self-evident, that all men are created equal, that they are endowed by their Creator with certain unalienable rights, that among these, are Life, Liberty, and the pursuit of Happiness. That, to secure these rights, Governments are instituted among Men, deriving their just powers from the consent of the governed, that—whenever any Form of Government becomes destructive of these ends, it is the Right of the People to alter or to abolish it, and to institute new Government, laying its foundation on such principles and organizing its powers in such form, as to them shall seem most likely to effect their Safety and Happiness. Prudence, indeed, will dictate that Governments long established should not be changed for light and transient causes; and accordingly all experience hath shown, that mankind are more disposed to suffer, while evils are sufferable, than to right themselves by abolishing the forms to which they are accustomed. But when a long train of abuses and usurpations, pursuing invariably the same Object evinces a design to reduce them under absolute Despotism, it is their right, it is their duty, to throw off such Government, and to provide new Guards for their future security. Such has been the patient sufferance of these Colonies, and such is now the necessity which constrains them to alter their former Systems of Government. The history of the present King of Great Britain is a history of repeated injuries and usurpations, all having in direct object, the establishment of an absolute Tyranny over these States. To prove this, let Facts be submitted to a candid world.

He has refused his Assent to Laws, the most wholesome and necessary for the public good.

He has forbidden his Governors to pass Laws of immediate and pressing importance, unless suspended in their operation till his Assent should be obtained; and when so suspended, he has utterly neglected to attend to them.

He has refused to pass other Laws for the accommodation of large districts of people, unless those people would relinquish the right of Representation in the Legislature, a right inestimable to them and formidable to tyrants only.

He has called together legislative bodies at places unusual, uncomfortable, and distant from the depository of their public Records, for the sole purpose of fatiguing them into compliance with his measures.

He has dissolved Representative Houses repeatedly, for opposing with manly firmness his invasions on the rights of the people.

He has refused for a long time, after such dissolutions, to cause others to be elected; whereby the Legislative powers, incapable of Annihilation, have returned to the People at large for their exercise; the State remaining in the meantime exposed to all the dangers of invasion from without, and convulsions within.

He has endeavoured to prevent the population of these States; for that purpose obstructing the Laws for Naturalization of Foreigners; refusing to pass others to encourage their migrations hither, and raising the conditions of new Appropriations of Lands.

He has obstructed the Administration of Justice, by refusing his Assent to Laws for establishing judiciary powers.

He has made Judges dependent on his Will alone, for the tenure of their offices, and the amount and payment of their salaries.

He has erected a multitude of New Offices, and sent hither swarms of Officers to harrass our people, and eat out their substance.

He has kept among us, in times of peace, Standing Armies without the Consent of our legislatures.

He has affected to render the Military independent of and superior to the Civil power.

He has combined with others to subject us to a jurisdiction foreign to our constitution, and unacknowledged by our laws; giving his Assent to their Acts of pretended Legislation.

For quartering large bodies of armed troops among us:

For protecting them, by a mock Trial, from punishment for any Murders which they should commit on the Inhabitants of these States:

For cutting off our Trade with all parts of the world:

For imposing Taxes on us without our Consent:

For depriving us in many cases, of the benefits of Trial by Jury:

For transporting us beyond Seas to be tried for pretended offenses:

For abolishing the free System of English Laws in a neighboring Province, establishing therein an Arbitrary government, and enlarging its Boundaries so as to render it at once an example and fit instrument for introducing the same absolute rule into these Colonies:

For taking away our Charters, abolishing our most valuable Laws, and altering fundamentally the Forms of our Governments:

For suspending our own Legislatures, and declaring themselves invested with power to legislate for us in all cases whatsoever.

He has abdicated Government here, by declaring us out of his Protection and waging War against us.

He has plundered our seas, ravaged our Coasts, burnt our towns, and destroyed the lives of our people.

He is at this time transporting large Armies of foreign Mercenaries to compleat the works of death, desolation and tyranny, already begun with circumstances of Cruelty & perfidy scarcely paralleled in the most barbarous ages, and totally unworthy the Head of a civilized nation.

He has constrained our fellow Citizens taken Captive on the high Seas to bear Arms against their Country, to become the executioners of their friends and Brethren, or to fall themselves by their hands.

He has excited domestic insurrections amongst us, and has endeavoured to bring on the inhabitants of our frontiers, the merciless Indian Savages, whose known rule of warfare, is an undistinguished destruction of all ages, sexes and conditions.

In every stage of these Oppressions We have Petitioned for Redress in the most humble terms: Our repeated Petitions have been answered only by repeated injury. A

The Declaration of Independence

Prince whose character is thus marked by every act which may define a Tyrant, is unfit to be the ruler of a free people. Nor have We been wanting in attentions to our Brittish brethren. We have warned them from time to time of attempts by their legislature to extend an unwarrantable jurisdiction over us. We have reminded them of the circumstances of our emigration and settlement here. We have appealed to their native justice and magnanimity, and we have conjured them by the ties of our common kindred to disavow these usurpations, which would inevitably interrupt our connections and correspondence. They too have been deaf to the voice of justice and of consanguinity. We must, therefore, acquiesce in the necessity, which denounces our Separation, and hold them, as we hold the rest of mankind, Enemies in War, in Peace Friends.

WE, THEREFORE, the Representatives of the UNITED STATES OF AMERICA, in General Congress, Assembled, appealing to the Supreme Judge of the world for the rectitude of our intentions do, in the Name, and by the Authority of the good People of these Colonies, solemnly publish and declare, That these United Colonies are, and of Right ought to be FREE AND INDEPENDENT STATES; that they are Absolved from all Allegiance to the British Crown, and that all political connection between them and the State of Great Britain, is and ought to be totally dissolved; and that as Free and Independent States, they have full Power to levy War, conclude Peace, contract Alliances, establish Commerce, and to do all other Acts and Things which Independent States may of right do.

And for the support of this Declaration, with a firm reliance on the protection of divine Providence, we mutually pledge to each other our Lives, our Fortunes and our sacred Honor.

Selected Bibliography

Montross, Lynn, *The Reluctant Rebels*, Harper Press, New York, 1950.
Nolan, Jeannette Covert, *The Shot Heard Round the World*, The Story of Lexington and Concord, Julian Messner, New York, 1963.
Scheer, George F., & Rankin, Hugh R., *Rebels and Redcoats*, The World Publishing Co., New York and Cleveland, 1957.
Selby, F. G. (ed.), *Burke's Speech on Conciliation with America*, Macmillan & Co., Ltd., London, 1961.
Schlesinger, Arthur M., *Prelude to Independence*, The Newspaper War on Britain, 1764-1776, Vintage, New York, 1965.
Wagner, Frederick, *Patriot's Choice*, The Story of John Hancock, Dodd, Mead & Co., New York, 1964.
Wright, Esmond, *Washington and the American Revolution*, Macmillan & Co., New York and London, 1958.

The literature on America's independence movement is legion. Periodicals and personal accounts of the events leading up to separation from Great Britain abound. The lives of the leading figures have been written over and over. The student can delve as deeply as he cares to into the pros and cons, the whys and wherefores, of independence. We have endeavored only to give the casual reader some feeling of the stresses and strains, the diversity of forces, that pressured Americans of two hundred years ago to revolt. Our scant bibliography is only a taste to tempt the student onward.

INDEX

Adams, John, 13, 14, 18-22, 38, 44, 63, 77, 78, 88, 89, 97, 101, 105-107, 111-114, 133, 135, 137-139, 144, 146, 149, 152, 154-159, 162-175, 179, 180
Adams, Samuel, 36, 37, 53, 69, 72, 75, 77, 78, 80, 88, 91, 94, 95, 99, 100, 102, 105, 108, 109, 125, 126, 130, 147, 159
Admiralty Courts, 68, 77, 78
Albany Congress, 16, 52, 107
Albany Plan of Union, 16
Allen, Ethan, 133, 168
America, American, 7, 8, 13, 14, 15, 19, 24, 52, 55, 58, 60, 61, 64, 68, 72, 75, 92, 132, 144, 147, 148, 150, 151, 159, 173, 175
American Colonies, 33, 34, (see also Atlantic Colonies)
American Philosophical Society, 16, 176
Amherst, Lord Jeffrey, 14
Annapolis (Maryland) *Gazette*, 26
Arnold, Benedict, 133, 152, 157, 168
Atlantic Colonies, 7, 9, 23, 40
Attucks, Crispus, 87, 88

Barré, Sir Isaac, 41, 42, 101
Bernard, Sir Francis, (Royal Governor of The Massachusetts Colony), 18, 35-36, 53, 62, 69-72, 74, 75, 78
Bland, Richard, 124, 131
Boone, Daniel, 103
Boston, 13, 14, 15, 18, 19, 21, 35, 37-38, 52, 58, 62, 64, 65, 68, 70, 72, 73, 75, 77, 78, 84-87, 91, 95-97, 99, 100, 101, 107, 110, occupation by British, 114-119, 122-123, 125, 127, 129-130, 134-135, 141, 145; British quit Boston, 149-150, 157
Boston Gazette, 36, 44, 52, 53, 69, 77
Boston "Massacre," 86-88
Boston "Tea Party," 93-97
Botetourt, Norbone Berkeley, Baron de, (Governor of Virginia), 79, 80
Bowdoin, James, 105
Braintree, (Massachusetts), 13, 18, 19, 21
Breed's Hill, 134, 135
Britain, British, Great Britain, British Isles, 7-10, 14, 16, 17, 22-25, 54, 55, 59, 63, 70, 104, 111-113, 129, 148, 151, 152, 154-155, 162, 167, 173, 175-177
British America, 24, 34
Bunker Hill, 9, 134-136
Burgoyne, Sir John, (General), 122, 157
Burke, Edmund, 61, 98, 123, 124

Canada, 17, 23, 24, 27, 133, 141, 150, 152
Carleton, Sir Guy, (Royal Governor of Canada), 141
Carolinas, The, 14, 16, 104, 172
Charles Town, Charleston, (South Carolina), 13, 17, 101, 131, 157
Circular Letter, of Boston Assembly, 72, 74, 99; of British Secretary of State, 72-73
Clark, Abraham, 169, 173
Clinton, Sir Henry, (General), 122, 157
College of New Jersey (Princeton), 106, 150, 169
Committee of Correspondence, 91, 97, 99, 101, 103, 105
Common Sense, 146-148
Concord, 9, 125, 129, 130
Condorcet, Marquis de, 178
Connecticut (Colony), 89, 106, 107, 110, 130, 133, 142, 146, 168
Continental Association, 113, 120
Continental Congress, First, 103-114, 118, 157
Continental Congress, *The* (second), 9, 119, 125, 130-165
Cushing, Thomas, 78, 109

Dartmouth, Earl of, (Secretary of State for the Colonies), 118, 119, 125

Index

Daughters of Liberty, 95, (see also p. 58)
Deane, Silas, 110, 130, 134, 146
Declaration of Independence, 10, 11, Act of Independency), 149, 152-153, 155-165, 172-180
Declaratory Act, 62, 71, 83
Delaware, 107, 157
Delawares (Indian Tribe), 25
Dickinson, John, 39, 40, 63, 70-72, 94, 106, 112, 114, 131, 136, 151, 152, 156
Dulany, Daniel, 120
Dunmore, John Murray, Earl of, (Royal Governor of Virginia), 100, 103, 130, 131, 137, 150
Dyer, Eliphalet, 107

Easterbrooks, Prince, 127
East India Tea Company, 94, 96
England, the English, 7, 8, 14, 21, 24, 27, 28, 29, 33, 53, 64, 67, 68, 73, 89, 104, 120, 144, 158
Essex (Mass.) *Gazette*, 97

Faneuil Hall, 13, 95
Fauquier, Francis, (Royal Governor of Virginia), 47, 51, 54
Florida, 24, 27, 151
Fort Ticonderoga, 133, 141, 145, 149, 152, 168
France, French, 7, 8, 14, 15, 16, 17, 24, 26, 54
French Sugar Islands, 17, 24
Franklin, Dr. Benjamin, 15, 16, 23, 37, 40, 43-44, 54, 61, 62, 67, 82, 97-98, 114, 132, 136, 138, 148, 152, 154-156, 159-162, 164-165, 168, 174, 180

Gadsden, Christopher, 55, 81, 107, 109, 150
Gage, Sir Thomas, (General), 63, 72, 85, 100, 110, 115, 116, 118, 119, 122, 123, 125, 126, 131, 134, 142
Galloway, Joseph, 108, 111, 132, 138
Gaspée, The (revenue vessel), 90, 91
George II, (King of Britain), 14, 18
George III, (King of Britain, Elector of Hanover), 18, 23, 24, 25, 26, 31, 33, 50, 54, 55, 56, 57, 59, 66, 72, 74, 80, 90, 110, 112-113, 118, 119, 136, 142, 143, 161-164, 173, 176, 177
Georgia, 54, 103, 120, 131, 172
Grafton, Augustus Henry Fitzroy, Third Duke of, 68
Grenville, George, 27, 33-35, 40-42, 56-57, 60, 67

Hall, Lyman, 131
Hancock, John, 19, 35, 36, 53-54, 59, 62, 72, 73, 77, 95, 96, 100, 117, 125, 126, 130, 132, 157-158, 160, 164, 168, 174, 178
Hancock, Reverend John, 19, 21
Hancock, Thomas, 19, 35, 36
Hamilton, Alexander, 121
Harrison, Benjamin, 104, 124, 160, 163-164, 170, 174
Harvard Hall, 35
Harvard University, 16, 19, 37, 71, 106
Henry, Patrick, 28, 30, 32, 45, 47-52, 79, 81, 91, 104, 108, 112, 124, 125, 130, 151
Hessians, (German mercenary soldiers), 9, 144, 145, 170
Hewes, Joseph, (Delegate to Continental Congress), 149
Hopkins, Stephen, 107
House of Burgesses, 28, 31, 47, 48-52, 81, 91, 104
House of Commons, 27, 40, 42, 48-49, 59, 60, 61, 67, 101, 106, 118
House of Lords, 40, 42
Howe, Lord William, (Major-General), 122, 134, 150, 157, 168
Howe, Richard, (Lord Admiral), 151
Huguenots, 14, 29, 41, 46
Hutchinson, Thomas, (Lieutenant-Governor of Massachusetts Colony), 18, 36, 53, 70, 74, 87, 90, 95, 98, 100

Independence (of the Colonies), 22, 23
India, 24
Indian, Indians, 7, 14, 15, 24-27, 94, 160
Ingersoll, Jared, 34, 39, 41

190 • INDEX

"Intolerable" Acts, (Coercive Acts), 101, 102, 110
Ireland, Irish, 14, 39, 61, 75
Iroquois, Six Nations of, 16, 160
Jay, John, 109, 132
Jefferson, Thomas, 29, 46, 47, 50, 51, 80, 91, 100, 104, 125, 136-138, 152-165, 169, 174-176, 178, 179, 180
Johnson, Samuel, 61
Kalm, Peter, 8
Knox, Henry, 145, 149

Lee, Charles, (Major-General), (Continental Army), 140, 142
Lee, Francis Lightfoot, 80, 104
Lee, Richard Henry, 80, 91, 100-101, 125, 135; and Independence Resolutions: 151, 155, 171
Lexington, 9, 125, 126, 127, 128, 130, 139
Liberty, The (sloop, merchant ship), 66, 73, 77
Lydia, The (sloop, merchant ship), 73
Lind, John, 178
Livingston, Philip, 107
Livingston, Robert R., 152
Locke, Dr. John, 21, 37, 70
London, 13, 19, 23, 26, 29, 36-37, 40, 59, 66, 68, 70, 72, 73, 75, 78, 79, 80, 81, 88, 100, 102, 114, 115, 118, 119, 122, 123, 141, 143, 156
Louis XIV, King of France, 24, 26
Lynch, Thomas, 107

Madison, James, 150
Maryland, 15, 16, 26, 58, 96, 104, 151
Mason, George, 62, 79, 81, 104
Massachusetts (Bay Colony), 13, 18, 21, 36, 44, 52, 53, 62, 64, 65, 69, 72, 74, 75, 76, 90, 91, 98, 99, 101, 102, 103, 106, 110, 111, 115-119, 123, 125, 129, 130, 140, 146, 149, 154, 168, 177
Mayflower Compact, 21
McKean, Thomas, 106, 158
Middleton, Arthur, 172
Minutemen, 117
Mississippi River, 24, 27, 33, 102

Mohawk (Indian Tribe), 94
Molasses Act of 1733, 17
Morris, Robert, 156
Morton, John, 107, 131
Mutiny Act (1764), 39, 63, 72

New England, 13, 16, 19, 20, 21, 52, 55, 58, 99, 108, 109, 117, 118, 122, 131, 134, 143, 144
New Hampshire, 54, 89, 108, 123, 140, 142
New Jersey, 15, 16, 54, 58, 64, 82, 96, 100, 106, 130, 151, 163, 166, 169, 177
Newport, Rhode Island, 57, 94, 142
Newport Mercury, 51-52, 68
Newton, Sir Isaac, 20, 21
New York, 13, 15, 34-35, 38, 39, 52, 54, 55, 58, 62-65, 68, 69, 72, 85, 89, 94, 95, 96, 101, 105, 106, 107, 109, 120, 123, 130, 132, 133, 135, 151, 156, 157, 166-168, 177
New York Gazette, 39
Non-Importation Agreement, (Associations), 81
North, Frederick, 8th Lord North and 2nd Earl of Guilford, 82, 83, 89, 92, 97, 98, 101-102, 116, 119, 122, 138, 151
North Carolina, 89, 149, 150

Olive Branch Petition, 136, 143
Oliver, Andrew, 52-53
Otis, James, 13, 18-22, 31, 36, 38, 52, 62, 69, 71, 78

Paine, Thomas, 98, 146-148, 150
Parliament (of Great Britain), 28, 34-35, 38, 40-41, 52, 54, 59, 62-65, 67-83, 92, 94, 99, 101, 110, 113, 119, 122, 123, 136, 139, 143, 144, 171
Peace of Paris, 24, ("Treaty of"), 26
Peggy Stewart, The (stamp ship), 96
Pendleton, Edmund, 124
Pennsylvania, 15, 16, 23, 25, 26, 39, 43, 58, 89, 103, 107, 108, 109, 111, 132, 148, 151, 156, 177
Philadelphia, 9, 13, 15, 39, 52, 61, 68, 70, 94-95, 101; First Congress convenes at, 103-114, 119; Sec-

Index

ond Continental Congress meets, 130-137, 142-144, 146-148, 151-175; Independence declared at, 176-177
Philadelphia, College of, 16
Philadelphia Gazette, (also *Pennsylvania Gazette*), 15-16, 43, 70, 94
Pitcairn, John (British Major), 117, 125, 128, 129
Pitt, William, Earl of Chatham, (Prime Minister of Britain), 17, 24, 27, 41, 57, 60, 62, 66, 68, 82, 101, 119
Pontiac (Indian Chief), 25-26
Poor Richard's Almanac, 15
Proclamation of 1763, (Proclamation Line), 25, 27, 34, 64

Quakers, 39, 58, 63, 70, 72, 107, 109, 148, 151, 155
Quartering Act (1764), 39, 65, 70, 101
Quebec, 18, 41-42, 112, 144, 150
Quebec Act, 102
Quincy, Samuel, 18, 19

Randolph, Edmund, 148
Randolph, Peyton, 30, 48, 49, 50, 80, 104, 108, 151
Regulators, 89
Revere, Paul, 36, 75, 87, 88, 99, 110, 116, 123, 125, 126
Rhode Island, 58, 91, 107, 142
Rockingham, First Marquis, (Charles Wentworth-Watson), 57, 59, 61, 66
Rodney, Caesar, 106, 157-158
Rutledge, Edward, 159, 163, 164, 171
Rutledge, John, 107

Scotch-Irish, 14, 15, 45
Seabury, Samuel, 120, 121
Senecas (Indian Tribe), 25
Seven Years' War, 24
Shawnees (Indian Tribe), 25
Sherman, Roger, 106, 152
Sons of Liberty, 33, 42, 44, 52, 59, 61, 62, 77, 85, 95, 105, 106, 116, 167
South Carolina, 13, 55, 107, 113, 123, 131, 150, 157, 159, 163
South Carolina Gazette, 81
Stamp Act, (tax), 42-44, 47, 48, 52-55, 57-65, 67
Stamp Act Congress, 52-55, 106, 108
Suffolk Reserves, 110, 111
Sugar Act of 1764, (Black Act), 37, 38

Thatcher, Oxenbridge, 18, 19, 52
Thomson, Charles, 108, 114, 156, 160, 161, 168, 170, 171, 174
Townshend, Charles, 42, 66-70
The Act (duties), 68, 71, 79, 83, 89, 92
Tryon, William, Royal Governor of North Carolina (earlier, of New York), 89

United Colonies, 10, 144, 145, 151, 155, 176
United States of America, 10, 154-155, 160, 174, 175, 176

Vermont, 133
Virginia, 16, 26, 28, 29, 31, 44, 45, 52, 54, 64, 79, 80, 81, 89, 91, 105, 113, 121, 124, 130, 134, 144, 148, 150, 151, 154, 164, 165, 171
Virginia Resolves, 81, 171

Ward, Artemus, 130, 134
Warren, Dr. Joseph, 36, 105, 127
Washington, D.C., 179
Washington, George, 26, 47, 64, 79, 81, 104, 109, 114, 125, 134, 135, 140-142, 145, 149, 156-157, 163, 168, 171, 177, 178, 180
Westchester Gazette, The, 120
Wilkes, John, 56, 118
William and Mary College, 29, 30, 46-47
Williamsburg (Va.), 46, 79, 100, 130
Wilson, James, 132, 151, 159, 169
Winthrop, John, 16
Witherspoon, Dr. John, 106, 150, 163, 169
Writs of Assistance, 17-22, 52, 68
Wythe, George, 47, 48, 50, 80, 104

Yale University, 39, 57, 71

About the Authors

Mary Hoehling was born in Worcester, Massachusetts, attended school there and in Noroton, Connecticut. After two years at Wheaton College, she left to marry A. A. Hoehling, the well-known author and settle in Washington, D. C. As she went through school, historic events and personalities captured her imagination. She began to write biography when her children complained of the dullness of history. She is the author of several published biographies for young people.

Betty Randall, a native of New York City graduated with a major in history from Vassar College. She earned an M.A. in anthropology at Columbia University and later qualified as a teacher. She has taught in high school, at the District of Columbia Teachers College and is currently training young people from the Washington, D. C. area for the job market in the General Studies Department of the Washington Technical Institute.